THE LOVING
RELATIONSHIPS TREASURY

SONDRA RAY

CELESTIAL ARTS
Berkeley | Toronto

Celestial Arts
an imprint of Ten Speed Press
PO Box 7123
Berkeley CA 94707
www.tenspeed.com

Distributed in Australia by Simon and Schuster Australia, in Canada by Ten Speed Press Canada, in New Zealand by Southern Publishers Group, in South Africa by Real Books, and in the United Kingdom and Europe by Publishers Group UK.

Cover and interior design by Lynn Bell, Monroe Street Studios
Cover art by fotosearch Stock Photography
Text compiled and edited by John Nelson

The material quoted from *A Course in Miracles* is used with permission from the publisher: Foundation for Inner Peace, PO Box 598, Mill Valley, California 94942, www.acim.org

For information on The Loving Relationships Training and Rebirthing worldwide:
    The New York and Philadelphia Rebirthing Centers
    c/o Tony Lo Mastro and Maureen Malone
    1027 69th Avenue
    Philadelphia, PA 19126
    (215) 424-4444 or (212) 534-2969
    tony.lomastro@verizon.net or maureenmalone@earthlink.net
For more information about Sondra Ray, visit www.SondraRay.com

Library of Congress Cataloging-in-Publication Data on file with the publisher.

ISBN-13: 978-1-58761-274-9
ISBN-10: 1-58761-274-7

First printing, 2006
Printed in the United States of America

1 2 3 4 5 6 7 8 9 10/ 10 09 08 07 06

CONTENTS

Introduction: The New Paradigm *vi*

CHAPTER 1 THE PURPOSE OF LIFE AND RELATIONSHIPS 1
Clear Up Your Relationship with God *3*
Get Enlightened *5*
Live Enlightened *7*
Knowing the Purpose of Life *9*
A Sacred Partnership *11*

CHAPTER 2 THE NATURE OF RELATIONSHIPS 13
Love Yourself, Heal Yourself *15*
People Treat You the Way You Treat Yourself *17*
Get Rebirthed Frequently *19*
Commitment to Purification *22*
Discarding Old Models *25*
Being with an Equal *27*
Needing A Sense of Balance *30*

CHAPTER 3 RELATIONSHIP PHASES AND ADJUSTMENTS 32
Attracting a Mate *35*
Knowing What You Want from a Relationship *37*
The Interview *39*
Relationship Phases and Adjustments *41*
Patterns *45*
Going for Total Enlightenment *48*
Having a Spiritual Mission Together *50*

CHAPTER 4 DAY-TO-DAY RELATIONSHIPS 52
Clean Up Relationships Daily *54*
Find the Highest Spiritual Thought *56*
Problem Solving *59*
Mind Tracks *67*

CHAPTER 5   RELATIONSHIP DYNAMICS 72
          The Illusion of Ego 74
          Communication 77
          Double Messages: The Yes-No Problem 80
          Have the Right Attitude 83
          Conforming and Rebelling 85
          Problem Solving in the New Paradigm 87

CHAPTER 6   RELATIONSHIP CLEARING 90
          Getting Yourself Unstuck 92
          Taking Responsibility 94
          Give Up Guilt 96
          Basic Forgiveness Affirmations 98
          Assisting in the Clearing Process 99
          Taking Care of Your Relationship 105
          Keeping Your Relationship Clear with Everyone 109

CHAPTER 7   ADVANCED RELATIONSHIP DYNAMICS 111
          Your Space and Environment 114
          Money and Relationships 119
          Giving and Receiving Feedback in the New Paradigm 123
          Sex in the New Paradigm 127
          Marriage 129
          Children 134

CHAPTER 8   RELATIONSHIPS IN TRANSITION 139
          "First-Aid" for Your Relationship 141
          The Fear of Change 144
          The End of a Relationship 148
          Letting Go without Bitterness 150

CHAPTER 9   SPIRITUAL DYNAMICS IN RELATIONSHIPS 153
　　　　　Handling Karmic Debts and Dues *155*
　　　　　Transmuting Upsets *158*
　　　　　Maintaining Respect *161*
　　　　　Blessing Instead of Judging *163*
　　　　　Devotion: Worshipping Together as a Couple *166*
　　　　　The Goal of Stabilization of Bliss *168*

CHAPTER 10   SPIRITUAL RELATIONSHIPS 170
　　　　　Holy vs. Unholy Relationships *173*
　　　　　A Course in Miracles on Relationships *177*
　　　　　Intimacy with Everyone *189*
　　　　　A Community of Majesty *191*
　　　　　A Life of Service *193*

CHAPTER 11   ADVANCED SPIRITUAL DYNAMICS IN RELATIONSHIPS 195
　　　　　The Whole Woman *198*
　　　　　Especially for Men *200*
　　　　　Surrender *202*
　　　　　Encouragement and Gratitude *204*
　　　　　Divine Control *206*
　　　　　Divine Love *208*
　　　　　The Highest Reality *211*

APPENDIX   THE IMMORTAL RELATIONSHIP 213
　　　　　The Death Urge in Relationships *214*
　　　　　Physical Immortality *219*
　　　　　The Immortal Couple as a New Paradigm *226*
　　　　　Index *228*

INTRODUCTION: THE NEW PARADIGM

The New Paradigm is the paradigm of joy. It is the unholy relationship made holy, with gratitude and praise being the building blocks to mutual bliss. But the New Paradigm begins with *you*. You cannot remain stuck in old patterns and habits and expect to create new, healthy relationships.

So let's talk about finding a mate in the New Paradigm. The first key is to be happy with your self before trying to find someone else to be happy with. It is a myth that there is someone out there who will complete you. Only *you* can complete you. People do not change each other; they only change themselves. Being in a holy relationship will inspire you to be your highest self. Being in an unholy relationship will drive you further away from your highest self, and eventually from each other.

The second key is to pray to God and the Masters to find the right person for you. You can go on my website and do the *kahuna* prayer I wrote for finding a mate. I have received so much great feedback from people who have had wonderful results. Surrender yourself and your prayer into God's hands and even if you feel like you are not quite ready, trust me, God will make you ready! It also helps to prepare your living space for a new relationship. One of my friends once said to me, "People deserve to live in gentle, loving environments, where aliveness, delight, and joy are the norm. Anything less is an insult to the human spirit." I love this statement. Prepare every room for God and your new mate will feel welcome, too.

The third key is to devote energy to your spiritual path. If your goal is to attract a mate who is ready to handle the New Paradigm, then you *both* must have an equal commitment. Of course, this begins with *you*. If your commitment isn't whole hearted, you cannot expect your mate to be fully committed.

Each relationship is, in fact, a spiritual workshop. My favorite definition for a New Paradigm relationship is from Gary Zukov's book, *Seat of the Soul*. He calls it a Spiritual Partnership in which you are together for the evolution of your souls and you are committed to each other's spiritual growth. Another definition I like is this: a holy interpersonal environment for the evolution of two souls who are aware of the deeper reason they are together, who take the time to allow a higher vibration to flow through them, and make equality and wholeness a way of life.

What are the qualities of this New Paradigm relationship?

First and foremost it is continuously transforming. It is about movement and growth as the couple constantly shifts from the old mentality of inferiority versus superiority, to one of equality and balance. The traditional roles of domination and submission cease and true cooperation can exist between people who are consciously breaking old destructive patterns and habits.

Of course, transformation and growth aren't possible without clear, honest communication. As men and women find their voices and allow themselves to articulate their feelings, couples are empowered to fearlessly reveal their deepest doubts and most fundamental needs. The ability to communicate is the cornerstone of being able to solve problems, which can be a stumbling block for even the most enlightened couples. Here are some important points about communication in the New Paradigm: Set aside a private time to create a safe time and space with no interruptions. Always use a calm tone of voice and use compassionate phrasing, such as: "What I feel is . . . " or, "What

I need is . . ." Remember, you can disagree without becoming upset. Just because you disagree doesn't mean you've stopped loving each other. Also, no withholding; no secrets; no silent treatments. Without trust, you have nothing. Do not interrupt each other and truly listen. Don't rehearse your rebuttal while the other person is speaking. Remind yourselves that you are both "on the same side." Keep going until there is satisfaction, even if you need to take a break to get there. This may mean letting go of a position, but always be willing to go for the highest spiritual idea, no matter who "wins." Know when you are stuck and use spiritual practices to get clear; if necessary, get a third party to help you negotiate fairly. Because men and women are "hardwired" differently, self realization techniques are the essential "software" that a couple may use to reenergize their commitment and find their way back to each other and to God.

In closing, it is so important to mention the attitude of gratitude. Some people say "I will be grateful when . . . ," But this does not work. Be grateful for whatever you have and for whatever is unfolding for you *right now* even if it is not what you think you wanted. Try telling people this: "I am grateful that you exist," and see what happens! Appreciation is one of the highest vibrations and has a truly healing effect.

Love, *Sondra Ray*

Postscript: Because this book contains excerpted material selected from my previously published books, *Loving Relationships, Loving Relationships II,* and *Creating Sacred Relationships,* certain passages and concepts have been repeated.

CHAPTER 1

THE PURPOSE OF LIFE AND RELATIONSHIPS

Relationships are how most people process themselves and help each other along the path of enlightenment. The first, and most important, step is to be clear about your relationship to God. You may need to examine your beliefs in regard to God, since all of us bring a huge amount of conditioning to this prime relationship. Hopefully, you will come to realize, as I have, that you must maintain oneness with God to be grounded in your being. That is because God's power courses through you, pours energy into your thoughts and desires. And like God you are the creator of your own world.

If you are unaware of this power, and something terrible happens to you or your relationship, you won't take responsibility for it. You may even blame God for your misfortune. Such negative thinking can take hold of us from birth. A negative birth experience can create trauma that lasts a lifetime. That is why it is important to realize that we create our reality. Otherwise, we blame ourselves or our partners for every misstep along the way. If both partners are enlightened, any problem can be resolved.

When both partners truly know themselves as individuals, it is natural for them to want and to create a holy relationship. *A Course in Miracles* teaches us that we must immediately dedicate our relationships to the Holy Spirit. To enter and maintain such a relationship, we must commit ourselves to spiritual purification together. As Ram Dass says, "Why are we here? You are here to take the curriculum." You can let life be your teacher or, as I've discovered, practicing purification techniques is faster and easier.

This doesn't have to be rigorous and painful. As Robin Williams' mother told him as a child, the purpose of life was to experience intense joy. I would add that you are here to learn, clear your karma, serve humanity, dissolve the ego, and as my gurus in India tell me, to recognize the Supreme. The purpose of our relationships is to enhance these goals. Everyone is a candidate for total enlightenment.

In a sacred partnership, each must understand that the most profound reason they are together is for the evolution of their souls. A relationship should be about growth and movement. Each partner should want the other to become all that he or she can be and shouldn't feel threatened by this desire. But, a cautionary note, as *A Course in Miracles* points out, is to beware of using a special relationship as a substitute for God. In the new paradigm, we have a mystical purpose that transcends the personal needs of each partner.

CLEAR UP YOUR RELATIONSHIP WITH GOD

If you want your personal relationships to work, you must get clear on your relationship to God. When you're clear about who (or what) God is, then you have all the help you need for your relationships. If you aren't clear about God, you may try to blame God for your troubles; you may even think that God punishes you or is out to harm you.

God is the Source from which everything and everyone arises. If you don't have a good relationship with the Source, how can you have a good relationship with people? How can you love someone when you don't love the Source?

To have a good relationship with God, you must have some understanding of God, and God has always been a difficult concept for people to grasp. You may have felt confused about God, and you may have also felt guilty as you searched for the truth, especially if you had a strong childhood background in an orthodox religion. It may seem disloyal to your parents and religious teachers to consider breaking away from the creed they taught you as a child. However, such a search doesn't have to be a denial of those beliefs but can enlarge upon your childhood conceptions and actually strengthen them.

Maybe you've tried to run away from God, but how can you run away from your Source? You must maintain your oneness with God in order to be grounded in your own being. God lets you find yourself. Another way of putting this is that God allows you to work out your own salvation.

God is the Great Affirmative that always says "Yes" to your thoughts; God is energy added to your thoughts. If I say, "I am going to die when I am around seventy," God says, "Yes, if that is what you want," and adds more energy to that thought. When we become clear that thought is creative, we can say, "I am giving up the thought that death is inevitable and I am *youthing*!"

As soon as we know that we have all of God's power available to us—as much as we can take—then everything changes. We can love God! We don't have to fear surrendering to God, because we know that God is not out to harm us.

The truth is that you are the Source, and part of the Source. In other words, you and the Source are inseparable. All your relationships are determined by you; you can have them however you want them, because God the Source pours energy into your thoughts and desires.

GET ENLIGHTENED

Once *both parties* are enlightened, anything can be resolved. Until then it is often difficult, if not impossible, because of negative thinking. Your thoughts produce results even though you're no longer consciously aware of them. If something terrible happens to you, you might have trouble taking responsibility for creating it, if unaware of the negative thought that originally created the situation. That is why it's so important to bring up and clear out negative thinking.

An example of a thought from birth that can destroy relationships is one which many women accepted the moment they were hung upside down and hit on the bottom by a male obstetrician: "Men hurt me."

Since the thinker is creative with his or her thoughts, this thought begins to produce results very early for a little girl. In kindergarten boys act out her beliefs by knocking her down or hitting her. She is teased by boys in grade school. Then in high school she starts dating and finds herself jilted because she still has the thought in her subconscious.

After a childhood and through the teenage years of creating abuse from boys, she enters adulthood certain that men will hurt her. When a man comes along who seems to be nonthreatening, she lays aside her anxieties and recovers long enough to fall in love and get married. When that doesn't work out and her husband runs off with her best friend, the old belief that "men hurt me" is reinforced, and she resolves to have nothing further to do with men. All the time, the males in her life were simply acting out her lifelong subconscious belief. She herself, of course, was not even conscious of it.

Obviously, women act out men's thoughts in just the same way. A thought originating at birth for many men is that "Women want to suffocate (kill) me." Women may act this out by being too maternal and overprotective. Men usually interpret this as a sign that the women are trying to trap them. Thoughts create reality.

The way to rid ourselves of these destructive subconscious thoughts is to identify them by careful examination and use affirmations to uproot and heal the negative thinking.

Live Enlightened

When we rescind our egos and dedicate our love to do something greater than ourselves, relationships bloom. *A Course in Miracles* teaches us that we must *immediately* dedicate our relationships to the Holy Spirit if we want them to work (paraphrase, Text, pp. 337–338). When both people in a relationship truly know themselves as individuals, it is natural for them to want and to create a holy relationship. When they commit to spiritual purification together as a way of life, the vitality and joy arising from their partnership is truly amazing. The union is strengthened when both partners are committed to holiness and service to humanity above all else. When the relationship is about supporting each other toward that purpose, the excitement of synergy and expansion surpass all boundaries.

Relationships teach us and force us to grow, expanding our identity outward. When partners follow the right track, they soon yearn to join together with other enlightened people, pooling their collective energies to make a real difference in the world. Once they team up with others, they will very likely want to create a "spiritual family" where everyone is working together sharing the light.

As Terry Cole Whittaker, former Science of Mind minister, once said, "Life itself is an ashram and every moment is a spiritual opportunity." Many people have had their armor broken down by life's troubles and have become spiritually developed during the course of their trials. I have had both experiences. I've let life itself be my teacher, taking what comes, and I've consciously practiced spiritual purification techniques which break down the ego. I have found the second way faster and easier. I have listed the purification techniques I recommend in my book *Pure Joy*.

The spiritual master Saibaba tells us that "the sole purpose of your incarnation is the crucifixion of the ego . . . to grow in love, to expand that love, and to merge with God and this is best done through service." I also like Ram Dass's ideas on this subject:

> Why are you here? You are here to take the curriculum. You can use your own 'case' [your negativity, anger, lust, fear, and so on] as a stepping stone . . . from somebodiness to nobodiness; when you are nobody you are free to be everybody and everything.

All over the globe today, wondrous and unexpected discoveries about life's purpose are being brought to light by brilliant thinkers of our era. We would do well to keep abreast of them. Ken Carey, author of *Terra Christa, the Global Spiritual Awakening* is one of these great thinkers. The profound significance of Carey's revelations has no limit.

Never should an aspect of identity that perceived itself as separate from God dictate behavior.

Think about it!

KNOWING THE PURPOSE OF LIFE

I read once that Robin Williams' mother told him as a child that the purpose of life was to experience intense joy! (Imagine having a mother like that!) My gurus in India believe that the purpose of life is to recognize the Supreme. They understand that we're here to learn to recognize ourselves and others as part of the Supreme God. Knowing who you really are leads to intense joy.

A third purpose in life is to learn. Our world is a school and we must never stop being students in it. Learning includes changing, and expanding.

A fourth purpose in life is to clear your karma. If you want to know more about that subject, read books like *We Were Born Again to be Together* by Dick Sutphen, and *Other Lives, Other Selves* by Roger Woolger.

A fifth purpose in life is to serve humanity. This is, and always will be, considered the first and foremost duty of the mature soul. This is called Karma Yoga.

A sixth purpose in life is the dissolution of the ego. This is a step-by-step process of giving up separation and limitation, which leads to the experience of ourselves as Divine Masters. This, in turn, leads to permanent liberation in which one transcends the human condition. One achieves permanent status in the Absolute.

In life, we experience a continuous push toward egolessness. A being has an intense desire to know its real self, to know the truth, the Eternal Source. Our overriding desire is to discover this source of infinite love and to express this love in daily life.

The purpose of the relationships is to enhance these goals. Both partners must share this intention, or they are missing the main point and will just have to keep dying and reincarnating until they get it!

Everyone is a potential candidate for total enlightenment; everyone has the blueprint. That is why we're here. Read *A Course in Miracles* for the most profound teachings of all on this subject. These books are the most important works in two thousand years.

A Sacred Partnership

In a sacred partnership, each partner is equally committed in assisting the other in his or her spiritual growth. Each must understand that the most profound reason they are together is for the evolution of their souls. This creates a whole new vibration between them.

A relationship should be about growth and movement. It should create a holy, interpersonal environment for the evolution of two souls. A relationship is a process; in that process, the couple should celebrate changes in themselves which are stimulated by one another. They should not resent the fact that the mate (the relationship) is encouraging them to change. Each should want the other to become all that he or she can be and should not feel threatened by this desire. In other words, you should not hold yourself back in any way, nor should you allow the other to hold you back. In fact, you should use the support of your mate to help propel you forward, to advance. Each should enjoy empowering the other, but neither should give away his or her power. Don't sell out—work it out!

I am describing intimacy as a path. Strive for intimacy instead of intensity because intimacy leads to transformation. The power of intimacy brings up all of one's fears to be processed. You must first want to become enlightened so you can make the relationship work for you. Then you must eliminate all barriers to expressing your love.

Beware of using a special relationship as a substitute for God. This is most important to understand. *A Course in Miracles* says that "A special relationship is the ego's chief weapon to keep you from God." So, if you are spending all your time and energy (as most people do) trying to make a relationship work with someone who you think is more special than you or anyone else, it will never work.

In the new paradigm, we must have a mystical purpose that transcends the personal needs of the two people in the relationship. This requires a partner who is willing to work with you on forming a triangle with God. That is why I suggest you spend some time interviewing a person before you have sex with them. So what if the "interview" takes nine months? It has been recommended by the masters that you wait nine months before having sex anyway, if you really want your relationship to work. Otherwise you could be in grave danger of being led down the wrong road without even realizing it. Sex brings up everything and often too fast.

I am talking about a paradigm where two partners are striving for the spiritual adventure of exploring the higher possibilities of Spirit together. Ask yourself, are you willing to go that far?

CHAPTER 2

THE NATURE OF RELATIONSHIPS

If there is an axiom in relationship training, it's this: People Treat You the Way You Treat Yourself. This leads to one of my favorite definitions of love, as ultimate self-approval. I repeatedly tell people: you must become the right person rather than looking for the right person. Unfortunately, people hate themselves for a lot of different reasons, which more often than not can be traced back to strong negative thoughts at birth.

I am continually astonished by the effects of birth trauma on one's relationships later in life. Such difficulties as fear of entrapment, womblike dependency, fear of pleasure, and separation anxiety, are but a few. Rebirthing can permanently cure the fears that ruin relationships. Otherwise, once love begins to flow between two people, these thoughts will start to surface. Remember, love brings up anything unlike itself.

Keeping a "clear wave form," as José Arguelles calls it, means letting go of ~~such~~ fears which limit our ability to love and create in this time of turmoil and change. We must free ourselves to discover our own exceptional gifts and offer them for the common good. Our goal must be, as the Bible states, "Be ye perfect even as God is Perfect." But achieving inner mastery requires spiritual purification and the willingness to constantly change and improve ourselves.

In order to make a new paradigm work, one has to be willing to discard outmoded models. And while it's no longer appropriate to maintain a patriarchal society, our commitment should be to end all domination—period. Spiritual teamwork is the cornerstone for building such a paradigm together. Imagine men and women as full partners in running our society.

But you must first ask yourself: do you fear being with an equal? Are men afraid of giving up control, or being out of control, or if you're not in control, would she be? Are women afraid of their own power, to stand up and be themselves, or are they afraid of their real self? It's absolutely mandatory to clear such issues, because the energy created between two equals is astounding. It can be fun, exciting, but you'll both need to practice spiritual purification.

And while many blame the evils of today's world on such patriarchal values as competition, both men and women cooperated in creating this status quo. Feminism tried to address these issues and may have created a kind of course correction, but an imbalance still exists and it creates pain and confusion in our relationships. Power can only be shared when the third party is God.

LOVE YOURSELF, HEAL YOURSELF

I once knew a very beautiful woman who had everything, it seemed. But she was always fouling up her life, and she once lost everything including most of her wealth. She was a twin and had been born first and was the healthier of the two. Her sister, the second born, had always been sick and unsuccessful in life. My client hated herself because she thought she had ruined her sister's life by being born first. She ended up thinking, "I am a bad person." So, even though she was ravishingly beautiful, men stayed away because she didn't like herself; and she didn't treat herself well, feeling she should punish herself. (People treat you the way you treat yourself.)

Another woman hated herself because her sibling had died before she was born. She felt her parents really wanted that baby instead, and they had her to "make up for the loss." She felt she could never be who they wanted, and she hated herself. She too was a beautiful woman, but it didn't matter because she would always attract men who would beat her up in one form or another. She felt guilty for not being who her parents wanted, and she made sure to punish herself for it.

I've had many clients who hated themselves for not being the sex their parents had wanted. And the list goes on and on. People hate themselves for a million different reasons. People who hate themselves often get fat and then they hate themselves even more. Or they conjure up some other excuse to prove how bad they are.

It is very hard for them to heal their self-hatred unless they're aware of the strong negative thoughts they may have formed about themselves at birth or even in the womb. Self-hatred makes one ugly. I have seen people who gave up their self-hatred and forgave themselves become more and more beautiful right before my eyes.

People Treat You
the Way You Treat Yourself

Jesus said, "Love thy neighbor as thyself."

One definition of love is ultimate self-approval. If you love yourself, you will automatically give others the opportunity to love you. If you hate yourself, you won't allow others to love you. If your self-esteem is low but someone loves and accepts you, you will reject them, try to change them, or think they're lying to you.

When you blame the world for lacking love, you're creating still more negative mental mass, which makes it worse. Sometimes people tell me, "My life doesn't work because I don't have the right mate." That philosophy will never work. You must become the right person rather than looking for the right person. In order to attract the cream of the crop, you must become the cream of the crop.

Here are some other ways to increase your self-love:

1. Acknowledge and praise yourself to yourself.
2. Approve of all your own actions; learn from them.
3. Have confidence in your ability.

4. Give yourself pleasure without guilt.

5. Love your body and admire your beauty.

6. Give yourself what you want; feel that you deserve it.

7. Let yourself win—in life and in relationships.

8. Allow others to love you.

9. Follow your own intuition.

10. See your own perfection.

11. Let yourself be rich; give up poverty.

12. Reward yourself; never punish yourself.

13. Trust yourself.

14. Nourish yourself.

15. Let yourself enjoy sex and affection.

16. Turn all negative thoughts about yourself into affirmations.

P.S. High self-esteem is not being egotistical. "Egotism is trying to prove you're OK after you've fallen into hating yourself." (Marshall Summers)

GET REBIRTHED FREQUENTLY

In every Rebirthing I've ever done, I learned something new about the effects of the birth trauma on the individual's relationships later in life. I was continually astonished. One of the more drastic cases was a fellow named John. He was a breech baby. When he came out "butt first," his mother bled a lot and almost died. His conclusion, established at birth, was this: "In order to survive, I have to hurt someone, especially a woman." He had no memory of that decision, of course, but when he came to me, he was ready to kill himself and felt outright suicidal. His complaint was that he had a syndrome in which he kept hurting people, especially women. He said it turned him into a homosexual. (I am sure you can see the connection; when he was "inside a woman," she might die and this terrified him.) He had no recollection of his birth, and he felt Rebirthing would be the last thing he'd try before killing himself.

I remember that his Rebirth was long and deep and that he had a continuous flood of pictures and memories, including coming out breech, the blood, and his mother's near-death trauma. Once all these "connections" were made and I was able to design appropriate affirmations for him, he felt that he'd escaped this syndrome and now chose to live.

What does your birth experience have to do with your relationships? More than you ever dreamed! All of the following emotional responses are closely related to your birth:

1. Fear of entrapment in a relationship
2. Womblike dependency on a mate
3. Fear of pleasure
4. Separation anxiety
5. Fear of letting go with people
6. Fear of receiving love; distrust of people
7. Sexual problems
8. Poor self-image; feeling less confident than others
9. Feeling like you are dying when a partner leaves you
10. Suppressed anger and rage and more!

Our research has shown that the roots of these common problems can be traced back to the womb and the first five minutes of life. Before Rebirthing it was very difficult to re-experience the birth trauma that formed the personal laws that govern our lives. I like to say that this will likely be the first generation whose relationships really work by dealing with the birth-death cycle.

Rebirthing, not only can cure the fears that ruin relationships, but it also heals you in every way. As you breathe out negative mental mass retained from birth, you feel healthier, more alive, more beautiful, and more lovable. You naturally begin to attract healthier people into your life and find it easier to have loving, exciting relationships.

Some examples of the decisions I made at birth that had always affected my relationships with men were:

1. I can't love. It hurts. Life hurts.
2. I can't trust men, if this is what they're going to do to me.
3. Men can't be depended upon when I need them.
4. This is too much. I hate you. Stay out of my life.

With such thoughts it's a wonder I ever allowed any man to get close to me. At the beginning of a relationship, thoughts like this tend to be suppressed. But once love begins to flow, these thoughts start to surface. (This is because love brings up anything unlike itself.) Those subconscious thoughts would begin to rear their ugly heads and produce results, even though I was no longer consciously thinking them, and then the relationship would blast apart. (This usually happens when both partners' patterns are surfacing at the same time.)

Since I had buried thoughts from birth like "Men aren't there for me" and "Stay out of my life," having a man stay with me wasn't compatible with my programming. Therefore I'd have to create his leaving to support my pattern; it's like supporting a drug or alcohol habit. The men, even if they loved me very much, would run up against my pattern and were forced to give me what I expected—which was NOT being there.

A personal law (which we now call a personal lie) is that your most negative thought about yourself is usually formed at birth. You can see how important it is to become aware of your own personal laws, if you want it have good relationships.

COMMITMENT TO PURIFICATION

José Arguelles warns us that we have only until the year 2012 to get cleared. In his book, *Surfers of the Uvula*, he tells us that before that date we must become what he calls a "clean wave form." This means letting go of all old limitations, past-life fears, ego trips, competition, control, and separateness. Those destructive patterns, which limit our ability to love and create, must be abolished by then. Once we've done this, people with clean wave forms will be able to better manage the chaotic situation ahead.

As we strive to develop a clean wave form, we'll begin to discover our own individual and exceptional gifts. In case you feel uncertain whether you ought to invest your energy in this effort—let me be perfectly frank: discovering your particular path and contribution is your business on this Earth. I recommend you keep asking yourself the following questions: "What am I doing to create a unified global civilization that is living in harmony with nature?" "How can I contribute to that goal?" "How can I inspire all the people I know to work toward that goal?" Your answers could lead us toward global unity, the precursor to universal peace and the key to our very survival.

I've stated that the totality of our being is awesome. But just how awesome? The Bible gave us a very clear indication of our potential and purpose here on Earth: "Be ye perfect even as God is Perfect." This is our assignment. Achieving complete inner mastery means to become whole human beings striving for perfection in our *current form*.

Once we reach this level, we can aim for the next. We call this step *ascension*—a spiritualization process where even the physical body assumes qualities of the God within. During this process, the body's vibrations quicken until they merge with the inner light. Consequently, we are able to transcend death, dematerialize, and rematerialize. Such are the abilities of a true spiritual master.

If, as Shastriji (my guru) has said, the purpose of the human body is to recognize the Supreme, then we must also recognize that each of us is the Supreme, along with everyone else. That's because each of us has the potential to become a Supreme Spiritual Master; this quest is therefore our destiny, the destiny of every soul. If we don't achieve that goal during this life, we will come back and keep trying. Ascension is in fact the culmination of many lifetimes of effort dedicated to spiritual attainment.

By achieving ascension—the Bible calls it "overcoming"—we must rise above ego delusions, disharmony, and death. Ruby Nelson's wonderful book, *The Door of Everything*, spells out this idea clearly. Nelson explains that if you have not handled your lower nature and death urges, your body will not tolerate the light vibrations of ascension. Physical immortality must be achieved before we can handle the light of dematerializing and rematerializing our bodies.

Discovering the purpose of your life will require your willingness to constantly change and improve yourself. You'll need to clear yourself through spiritual purification, to work out your karmic debts, and to resolutely fulfill your own divine life plan. Making spiritual purification a regular practice in your life not only works, it makes you ecstatic. And if you do these practices with another person, your relationships are filled with vitality and love.

DISCARDING OLD MODELS

For a new paradigm to work, one has to be willing to discard the outmoded models first. But what if we are attached or even addicted to those models? What if one feels strongly about an outmoded model out of loyalty to one's parents or to one's culture? For example, learning a model of masculinity from their fathers might make men mistrust any new model of maleness presented to them out of a sense of disloyalty. I once read an article in which family therapist Frank Pitman made this statement:

"Trying to teach a man with an outmoded model of masculinity to be an emotionally sensitive equal partner to a woman, is much like trying to teach a pig to sing!" (Pitman, 1994). How depressing! I was glad a man wrote that! But it isn't impossible to change.

Women have similar problems. If a woman does actually prefer an overpowering man, she may unconsciously want to keep the old patriarchy intact. She probably won't recognize how this hurts society, herself, or her children. Women are often afraid to become all they can be. It sometimes seems easier or more comfortable, in one sense, to give their power away to men and simply live with the old, outmoded forms. I assure you, this will not last—sooner or later they'll become fed up!

It's no longer appropriate to maintain a patriarchal structure in our society; but that doesn't mean we want to return to a matriarchal system either. We must all commit to the end of resentment, destruction, and bad health—we must commit to the end of domination—period.

Coupled men and women have to see the importance of this new paradigm; they have to be equally willing to release old models, and they have to be committed to overthrowing generations of negative conditioning. This requires transformation. This requires doing the work of transformation on oneself. Spiritual teamwork becomes the cornerstone for building the new paradigm together. It cannot be omitted. It has to be an integral part of one's daily life. It has to be a top priority.

BEING WITH AN EQUAL

Imagine this: Men and women as full partners in running society. It's going to happen. In fact, the partnership has already been set in motion. Why not join in now? Why not be a part of this exciting idea?

Do you fear having an equal? Begin to process your truth by answering these questions:

MEN

1. Are you afraid of giving up control?
2. Are you afraid of being out of control?
3. Are you afraid that if you're not in control, she would be?
4. Are you afraid of someone standing up to you? Are you afraid of feedback?
5. Are you afraid of facing yourself?
6. Are you afraid she will become your mother?
7. Are you afraid you won't be able to do everything you want to if you don't make all the final decisions?
8. Are you afraid of being disloyal to your father's patterns?
9. Are you afraid of change in yourself?

10. Are you afraid of the energy, the synergy, the possible excitement of creativity?

What ARE you afraid of?

WOMEN

1. Are you afraid of your own power, of standing out?
2. Are you afraid you'll be lost without someone controlling you?
3. Are you afraid to stand up to a man and be yourself?
4. Are you afraid of your real self?
5. Are you afraid you cannot make it on your own, so you'd allow yourself to be controlled rather than being alone?
6. Are you afraid of being different than your mother?
7. Are you afraid you cannot do it anyway? You are not as good as a man?
8. Are you afraid people will criticize you if you're different?
9. Are you afraid you won't be able to keep the peace unless you give your power away and give in?
10. Are you afraid of the energy, the excitement, the aliveness of it all?

What ARE you afraid of?

It's our task to give up and get over our fears. Accepting this responsibility is part of becoming enlightened. It's absolutely mandatory that you work out methods of clearing, because if you do find an equal, you'll have to deal with an upsurge of energy. This energy between equals is very intense—just the sheer *life* of it will bring up anything unlike itself. So you'll have to understand conflict resolution and will need to know how to handle your unconscious behavior. Equal partnership can be fun—if you both agree to it and if you both know spiritual purification techniques.

Don't deprive yourself of the excitement of having an equal!

Needing a Sense of Balance

Many people believe the evils of today's world can be blamed on the six-thousand-year-old reign of patriarchal values as seen in warfare and competition and male domination. But it is too easy to blame the patriarchy alone. It is important to look at the effects of what both sexes have co-created in our society. Shouldn't we be working toward the end of *all* domination? After all, some men feel victimized by women too! Remember, one sex is not victimized by the other. THERE ARE NO VICTIMS. *A Course in Miracles* clearly teaches this: "There is nothing that happens without you calling for it, or asking for it."

Mary Daly, author of *Beyond God the Father*, points out that the model of the universe in which a male God rules the cosmos serves to legitimize male control of social institutions. She further states that, "The unconscious model continues to shape the perceptions even of those who have consciously rejected archaic religious teachings. The details of one's dogma are rejected, but the underlying structure of belief is imbedded at such a deep level it is rarely questioned" (Daly, 1985).

Therefore a system cannot simply be rejected, it must be *replaced*. We must all take responsibility for this development and not blame men. In fact, many of us women could've been in past lives the very men who perpetuated this pattern! Scott Peck says, "We live in an oversexualized culture and undoubtedly the greatest burden of that is borne by women. Not simply as victims though. Men have been accused of treating women as sex objects . . . but women are the first to treat themselves that way . . . they are really out of kilter [in] the way they focus on their bodies. Women are held back by their own fear."

Many women feel that, in order to operate with any effectiveness in our culture, they have to immerse themselves in the values of male-dominated society. Many women don't trust their own truths because they grew up trying to please men. Feminism tried to address these issues but many women now feel unable to manage their spiritual paths and be in a loving relationship with a man. We must all face the fact that this imbalance is causing pain in our relationships, in our families, and in society. That is the reason we must all think about it . . . without any blame.

If we aren't in balance with the male and female sides of ourselves, we will experience conflict in our own minds. Resolution has to happen within us first. But don't be surprised if you then attract fights with the opposite sex!

This power struggle is no fun and creates a lot of confusion. Some women cannot stand feeling oppressed and powerless in a relationship. Other women may actually prefer an overpowering man. Some men feel lower self-esteem living in the shadow of successful women. Other men are *only* attracted to strong, independent women! We *all* have to get our priorities straight and give ourselves, and each other, time and space in which to do that.

RELATIONSHIP PHASES AND ADJUSTMENTS

CHAPTER 3

The person you're looking for will show up if you think the right thoughts and let go of any resistance. Walking around thinking "I'll never find anybody" will chase people away. Your thinking *does* produce results.

Once you've found them, how do you make the relationship thrive? Having a similar vision of the relationship is the key. Do you both want the same things: comfort and security, sexual satisfaction, or are you looking for a business partner? What if you both decided that you wanted what was in your highest interest, even if that was facing your shadows? Relationships are a test of your spiritual qualities. Your mate is your guru.

With that in mind, you might, as I do, start to "interview" your potential mates. What is the purpose of the relationship, what is your top priority, do you feel the same about God? You can't be afraid to "put it out there." It's risky, but why fall madly in love with someone who doesn't share your visions or goals? That is a recipe for disaster.

We enter relationships compelled by various attractions. There's the obvious sexual attraction that can overwhelm one's judgment, and you find yourself bound to someone who doesn't satisfy all your needs. Karmic attractions are rooted in past lives, whereas cosmic ties bring together evolved individuals to perform a special service. Relationships are critical for spiritual development. Be aware of all the implications before "diving in."

Whatever the attraction, the relationship will bring up what I call "Repetitive Unconscious Behavior," based on our family blood line or reactions to those behaviors. For example, the attractions we experience to both our parents set models by which we judge potential mates. This is a very deep and complex pattern that can take years for people to work out. It can explain why the minute some people get married that their sex drive diminishes. Remember, love will attract everything unlike itself to be cleared.

Faced with such a quagmire, the obvious solution is to strive for enlightenment. There are no halfway measures. *A Course in Miracles* describes it as choosing the Holy Spirit's thought system instead of the ego's. An enlightened couple knows the difference and is vigilant against ego drives based on separation, guilt, fear, pain, and suffering. Another definition is taking responsibility for all the results in your life all of the time.

A higher purpose can also defuse the ego and take a relationship to another level.

Imagine if couples sat down and decided, right from the beginning, what kind of mission they were going to accomplish together for the world—*and then actually did it*. Do you think they'd get caught up in petty squabbles? If love has waned and the relationship is stale, it might be due to a lack of common purpose.

ATTRACTING A MATE

It's very easy to attract a mate if you think you can! If you understand a little metaphysics, the days of worrying and hoping and looking in bars are over. There is such a thing as the "Universal Metaphysical Law of Attraction." I prefer to call it "The Cosmic Dating Service." It always works, if you let it. You don't have to worry about the where or the how. The person you're looking for will show up anywhere, when and only when you are ready. You merely have to think the right thoughts and let go of any resistance you have to receiving.

The mistake that most people make is forgetting that their thoughts produce results *all the time*. People walk around thinking, "I'll never find anybody" or "There aren't any available men (women) around here." Or "Nobody ever asks me out," and then they wonder why they're home alone! Especially after a breakup, the person "left behind" usually ends up thinking something like "I'll never find anyone as good as him (her)," "I'll never make it alone," or "My life is over." All of these thoughts are destructive and produce negative results.

It's important to keep your heart open to receive. Then it is a matter of accepting and being certain that you deserve what you want. A good affirmation is "I am now willing to let into my life the man (woman) I desire." If you don't get a result after saying and writing this affirmation for a period of time, then you have a block . . . or what I call a "counter-intention." You have a sabotaging thought buried somewhere, and you must find it. This can be uncovered and released easily by using most affirmation techniques.

You will attract mates (actually you attract everyone in your life with your thoughts; this applies to attracting clients, business partners, and friends) who fit into your family patterns. After you understand and become cleared of those patterns, you will automatically attract someone who is in harmony with your highest thoughts and life will be easy.

KNOWING WHAT YOU WANT
FROM A RELATIONSHIP

I have read that researchers from the University of Arizona found that the secret to lasting love was that couples shared a similar vision of the relationship. This is obvious in one sense, but how many people really discuss what it is they want from a relationship? What do you want?

1. Do you want comfort and security? (Does that mean you think differences should never come up?)

2. Are you looking for economic security? (Does that mean you think you cannot survive on your own?)

3. Are you looking for sexual satisfaction? (What happens if your sex life isn't satisfactory . . . is that grounds for divorce?)

4. Are you looking for a business partnership? (If so, you better tell the truth and remember that limited motives, such as sex and money, won't alone be satisfying.)

5. Are you looking for companionship? (Does it mean you are afraid of being alone? Or you cannot tolerate living alone? How can anyone else live with you if you cannot live with yourself?)

6. Do you think the purpose of life is to get married, have kids, and then die? (Have you never questioned traditional assumptions about life and relationships? Do you personally know what you want from life?)

What if you said that you want from a relationship whatever was in your highest best interest? And what if what was best was: To have all your dark shadows revealed and removed.

Of course, we all want our relationships to help us discover what life is like at its best. Who doesn't want that? But your dark shadows have to be removed first. Having a mate as a mirror is a powerful way to recognize them. A relationship is a test of all your spiritual qualities. Accept that your mate is your guru and your relationship is the best seminar you can ever take. That is the right attitude. Your partner will reflect all your patterns. Your relationship is an educational process. Therefore, you better talk about your expectations early on—the sooner, the better! From a spiritual point of view, your relationship will be a success if it's dedicated to truth, and determined by a mutual *vision of truth.*

You and your mate have to make your own map. You shouldn't assume that your purposes are aligned simply because you have common interests. I don't think it is good to wait until after your first sexual experience to discuss your intentions either. It may cloud your judgment as to what long-range qualities are needed in a committed relationship. Knowing when you can talk about such deep subjects is the test. It takes positive self-esteem to bring up these issues early.

THE INTERVIEW

Because my work requires constant traveling, I've often risked not bothering to get enough information about a man before I got involved with him. I just went with the flow, which was spontaneous and fun in one sense, but often resulted in disasters later. (I lived with one man for only one day!)

I decided to get smart. I started to question new male acquaintances: "How do you feel about God?" and "How do you feel about living forever?" I dared to ask these questions very early in the relationship. Their answers told me a lot about them. I thought my powers of discrimination were improving. I started meeting men who seemed very spiritual and who said they wanted to be Immortal. But they were not willing to act on their beliefs. They were, in fact, threatened by change, threatened by processing, and— worst of all—threatened by me! Since then, I have had to rethink and refine my approach. You have to know yourself and not be afraid to "put it out there." It takes a high degree of self-esteem to risk exposing yourself, but it's worth it. Why fall madly in love with someone who doesn't share your visions or goals?

You can begin interviewing a potential equal by finding out about his or her "relationship history." This usually reveals itself spontaneously. If it doesn't, make a conscious effort to uncover this information early in the relationship—as part of the getting-to-know-you stage. After that, if you're still interested, proceed with questions such as those below. (By the way, you don't have to ask them all in one night!)

1. What is your vision of the purpose of a relationship?
2. What are your top priorities in life?
3. Tell me how you feel about God? Goddess?
4. Tell me how you feel about living forever?
5. Are you willing to strive for total enlightenment? If so, does that mean you're willing to do the hard work, such as processing or spiritual purifications?
6. What is your method of problem solving? Do you retreat? Do you communicate?
7. What are your issues about money? About food? (If you are a vegetarian, you'd better talk about it—and a lot more. . . .)

This may sound calculating and unromantic, but if you avoid asking about your important issues, you'll probably regret it.

Try your interview in a romantic setting. Most importantly, always be aware of the danger that they may unconsciously try to please you and say what they think you want to hear. (You might do the same when they interview you!) In either case, answering without integrity will backfire later. We—you and I—*know* this to be true!

Relationship Phases and Adjustments

In an excellent article published in Australia's *Intent* magazine, Rob Tillet writes:

> When our attention is aroused by the presence of another energy field from another person, our chakras attempt to make a contact with this new field by preparing to receive and transmit energies. We are surrounded by an energy field that can occupy quite a space around our physical form. We are actually swimming in a field of energies.
>
> The essential nature of a relationship is energy exchange. When we meet a person for the first time, we are either attracted, repelled, or indifferent to him or her . . . according to the way in which an energy connection is established. Relationships consist of the exchange and mutual processing of energies. A healthy relationship is one in which the energy exchange is mutually beneficial to the participants. That would be called a *strengthening relationship:* one in which both of the partners is stronger as a result of the relationship than they would be without it. A *weakening relationship* is one

in which the energy exchange is actually destructive to the health and well-being of the partners.

When we form any kind of relationship, our chakras seek to connect with the appropriate chakra of the other person. When all chakras connect at the appropriate frequency, a dyadic, or totally fulfilling relationship develops.

The Esoteric Philosophy of Love and Marriage, by Dion Fortune, has the best explanation that I've found about why we attract the people we do attract. Dion Fortune states that souls can couple in three different ways:

- Through ordinary attractions of sex
- By renewing karmic ties
- According to higher cosmic laws

The Sexual Tie: Unfortunately, many people urged on by physical desire may resort to marriage with the first available partner. Often, they will erroneously rationalize their feelings by idealizing the object of their desire. Suddenly one day they realize they have bound themselves for life to a person who is incapable of satisfying any of their needs. Misery follows. This is a very important point: one's judgment can be clouded over completely when blinded by sexual desire.

The Karmic Tie: Bonds based on karma are less easy to distinguish. Karmic ties are rooted in attractions experienced in past lives. For a full discussion of this phenomenon, I recommend you read the book *We Were Born*

Again to Be Together by Dick Sutphen for further information, and also *Other Lives, Other Selves* by Roger Woolger.

The Cosmic Tie: This is the most profound and potent tie. It is a partnership entered into by two individuals for the sole purpose of performing a special service; it's motivated by service alone. The partners in this union don't choose each other. They offer themselves for service to the Master on the Inner Planes. They're mated with attention to their qualities and capacities. The pair opens a channel. Divine forces flow through them with astounding power, magnetizing them and their surroundings. Through this union, the power of each partner is augmented; they are brought to their highest level of perfection.

After describing the different types of unions, Dion Fortune discusses the importance of mating on *matching planes*. [These are levels of development that we integrate through our spiritual journeys in one incarnation after another.] The first plane is the physical and material; the second is the lower astral; the third is the upper astral; the fourth is the lower mental; the fifth is the upper mental; the sixth is the lower spiritual; and the seventh plane is the upper spiritual. According to Fortune, unless we mate or align on each one of these planes, our union will be incomplete. For instance, if a man who has three developed planes marries a woman who has but two functioning, psychic and spiritual disaster can occur. Due to their negative effect on these inner planes, promiscuous sexual relations aren't taken lightly.

Fortune believes that we should take time before marrying to discover whether the relationship strengthens or weakens us. In a perfect marriage, Fortune writes, "the pair mate with each higher plane as it comes into function, applied to evolution: these two enter into the light."

An ideal union, of course, will often require a lengthy journey. As we make our way through the initial stage of a relationship—its conception—we must keep in mind that a new relationship means a *big change*. On the surface, this idea may seem obvious. But the fact that transitions tend to activate *birth trauma memories* is not so readily apparent. Tension rooted in these very early memories may mount very soon after your new relationship begins. The adage "Love brings up anything unlike itself" reveals another reason interactions can soon become rocky. In practical terms, your mate's love, which is a kind of energy, will purge you of anything unlike love—including guilt, fear, pain, doubt, the death urge, and so on. We might compare this to cleaning out a glass of water that has a layer of sediment on the bottom of it. As you pour in more water, the mud gets stirred up. The unexpected appearance of negative feelings—just when we think we have finally found a safe and loving relationship—may be very, very confusing. It will be important to note in advance, therefore, that the sudden appearance of negative feelings may indicate healing—not disintegration. It helps a great deal to have techniques like rebirthing to help you get through these phases of adjustment.

PATTERNS

When a couple survives the initial highs and lows of a budding relationship, they may consider making a commitment. If both want to be fully committed at the same time with the same degree of intensity, this stage can be very exciting. Often, however, a clumsy dance occurs in which one partner is more strongly committed, and the other less so: the old story of "When I want you, you don't want me. So I back off and don't want you, and then you want me." Some relationships survive this stage and some don't. It can be quite maddening, to say the least.

It is also important to understand that this is a *pattern*. A pattern is what we call "Repetitive Unconscious Behavior." Patterns are often based on repetitive behaviors in our blood families or reactions to those behaviors.

What motivates us to want someone obsessively when feelings of affection are not mutual—or vice versa? In examining cases like these, I've found that the "incest taboo pattern" can usually be found. This frustrating pattern begins during childhood. If you are female, you couldn't have your father, the man you really wanted. The way in which you cope with this disappointment is decided very early—and its effects continue into adult life. As an adult, when you can't have the one you really want because you have set him up as your father (or vice versa with the mother), that relationship then becomes "taboo" also.

This is a very deep and complex pattern. It often takes people many years to work it out. If we manage to suppress it enough in the beginning stages of the relationship, we may actually make a commitment and move in with or even marry a partner. But the incest taboo pattern, based on such a powerful impulse, usually surfaces sooner or later. The results can surprise and bewilder us. Some people actually find out that the minute they get married, sex no longer provides enjoyment or pleasure; others quickly disappear from the relationship altogether.

A relationship can generate a fantastic amount of energy when partners feel equal passion for one another. Yet maintaining an even balance is quite challenging. As I've explained earlier, "love brings up anything unlike itself," and passionate love frequently stimulates too many unconscious negative thoughts at once. A couple may become very happy, high, and passionate for days—then something inexplicable happens between them and suddenly the feelings disappear. Because negative subconscious thoughts have surfaced, partners need to know that this loss of passion is *natural* and *temporary*. Whenever it occurs, it's time to clear or process, and to practice spiritual purification. At such times, I say that the couple's "case came up." This means that the partners' birth trauma got activated, their unconscious death urge was stimulated, and their negative thought structures or family patterns surfaced. The tremendous love energy then produced pushed all these latent impulses outward. It is important not to get angry and give up at this time if you want to stay in this relationship. However, at this point, people often get disillusioned with each other, blaming each other for a waning romance. Ironically, this is just the moment when it is so crucial to have faith in yourself and your partner. It is a time to fortify the relationship with an enlightened understanding of how the mind works and do spiritual purification. If a couple gets rebirthed at this time, they can breathe out the subconscious material that has surfaced and then retrieve the love quite easily.

A crisis in your relationship can also provide an opportunity to develop a deep and mature love. This kind of bond celebrates our humanity—including our imperfections. By contrast, an immature love requires constant novelty; when the novelty declines, a new attraction is sought. Immature love needs a perfect idol as a love object. Lacking integrity, this kind of bond is frail and often shallow. But in a *mature love*—a relationship between two spiritual beings—a couple has the ability to weather love's unpredictable changes.

I can't emphasize how crucial it is for couples to develop spiritually enlightened methods of problem-solving and clearing during these early stages of a relationship. From the beginning, you'll need to discuss basic questions such as your purpose in life, your purpose in the relationship, what techniques you use to clear yourself, and how each of you can serve the other. Some people don't talk about these topics until it's too late, and bad habits have already formed. That's why honest discussion must begin immediately. Remember, there are people who not only tolerate, but require honest dialogue. Isn't this what you deserve? Seek them out!

GOING FOR TOTAL ENLIGHTENMENT

There are many different definitions of enlightenment. Any new paradigm for a relationship should emphasize the importance of agreement and commitment by both partners as they reach for their own definitions.

Leonard Orr, founder of Rebirthing, used to define enlightenment as "Certain Knowledge of the Absolute Truth" (i.e., knowing and remembering that your thoughts create your results). If one person in a relationship accepts this, but the other is not willing to consider the fact that his or her negative thoughts are producing negative results, how can the relationship work? The Bible states, "As a man thinketh, so is he" and "Thou art ensnared by the words of thy mouth."

An enlightened couple will constantly evaluate the results they get and study what thoughts and words brought about those results. They will evaluate what thoughts they need to change and will both work diligently to change them.

A Course in Miracles defines enlightenment as choosing the Holy Spirit's thought system instead of the ego's. An enlightened couple knows the difference and is vigilant against the ego. The ego is based on separation; the result is guilt, separation, fear, pain, struggle, misery, suffering, anger, depression, sickness, and death. The enlightened couple constantly works toward eliminating limited negative thoughts that lead to those ego states. Instead, they choose thoughts that are in keeping with the Holy Spirit's reality (i.e., union, life, love, joy, peace, harmony, health). The enlightened couple also knows that minds are joined and that each is a reflection of the other.

If you are operating in an enlightened paradigm, you will also understand and honor the following statements and how each applies to your relationship (also from the *Course*):

> You will attack what does not satisfy you to avoid seeing that you created it.
> Beware of the temptation to perceive yourself as unjustly treated.
> Only I can deprive myself of anything.
> There is nothing that happens without my calling for it or asking for it.

In other words: "Life presents to me what my thoughts are." This also means, of course, that blaming is off-kilter. In other words: "I am responsible for what I see, I choose the feelings I experience, and everything that happens to me I have asked for."

Being enlightened has to do with taking responsibility for all the results in your life all the time. The *Course* will tell you that all trials are lessons you failed to learn previously; you are always given another chance to choose again and do better.

The source of all of our experience is the mind. We rule and direct our minds and, consequently, we must change our thoughts to restore our mind to its full potential.

Having a Spiritual Mission Together

Imagine what would happen if a couple sat down and decided, right from the beginning, what kind of mission they were going to accomplish together for the world—*and then actually did it!* This spiritual mission could be a joint career. If they were already in different careers, they could still decide what kind of service they could offer the world together apart from their jobs.

When people are deeply in love, they feel a natural concern for the state of the world and they want to do something about it. If love has waned and the relationship is stale, it might just be due to the couple never acting on that sense of purpose. It is never too late to infuse your marriage or relationship with this gift. It is not only a gift to the world, but a gift to the relationship; it gives the relationship true meaning.

I have studied successful relationships of partners who were equally powerful. In fact, the equality in the relationship was part of the success. Bill and Hillary Clinton are a good example. They shared their commitment to public service before Bill became Governor of Arkansas. It is clear that this unity of purpose has helped them weather the storms of their marital life. They were focused on something greater than themselves. I think the American public has forgiven them their marital troubles because *everyone* has a past, and who wants a leader not tempered by life's lessons? Most importantly, I think we wanted to take the chance and experiment with equals running our country together. This is the new paradigm.

I read an article once called "100 Ways to Fix the World." The author interviewed one hundred famous people and asked them their recommendations. Filmmaker Eleanor Coppola said, "Every seven years, every able bodied should do three months of public service." This is a really good idea—for everyone! If you are single, you might meet the man or woman of your dreams while doing it.

Missions are satisfying. In my case, finding mine felt like the beginning of my true life. Everything before that was anticlimactic; I consider it like a past life. When I tell people what I was doing before I accepted and carried out my mission, they cannot believe that I'm the same person.

Once I held a class where each student selected a mission and then shared what they had chosen. Almost everyone totally underestimated their abilities—it was shocking! Choose something way beyond what you think you can do. This is called a "big stretch." Big stretches make you expand and, at the same time, they heal you. In my case, I needed help with relationships. I looked around, but in those days there were almost no seminars on relationships—not even in California! So I said, "Well, somebody has to study this . . . somebody should be teaching this—I guess it has to be me!" And that was how I first stretched to find my mission.

DAY-TO-DAY RELATIONSHIPS

CHAPTER 4

If you don't catch upsets when they happen, pretend to "get over" them and "stuff" the anger, it can lead to knock-down drag-out fights. I had a couple in a workshop stuck in this pattern. Finally, they agreed to clean up their relationship on the spot if possible, but at least every night before they went to bed. They kept their agreement and their relationship flourished. The amount of love that flows between the two people is often controlled by the quantity and quality of their communications.

Disagreements or "positions" can be best handled by finding the highest spiritual thought. You'll know it by listening to your body. The highest thought is always the most positive, the least limiting, and the most productive. When partners are willing to surrender their positions to the highest thought, they're not giving power away, they're creating a consensus. Harmony is always a winning position. And you can both work to upgrade the level of your thinking.

Otherwise, you will play out your family's behavior in regards to problem-solving dynamics. In family disputes, who gave their power away? What parent usually won and what was their strategy? Did the angriest parent force the other to cave in? Are you imitating these practices in your relationship? Arguments are no-win situations. Fighting is simply not an enlightened way of solving problems; it's a bad habit.

A Course in Miracles clearly states that anger can *never* be justified because "attack has *no* foundation." The first obstacle to peace, it adds, is "the desire to get rid of [peace]." But there are those who find peace boring and believe that life would be terribly dull without the "drama" of a troubled relationship. Or they believe that in their struggle to be creative that trials and tribulations are necessary, even desirable. The spirit of peace brings harmony to relationships and gives rise to tremendous creativity.

But some contemporary self-help books actually *encourage* us to fight; one author even asserts that those who don't fight don't care about life! Even therapists vehemently disagreed about the importance of releasing anger. One wanted to fight with me about the issue of fighting. I agree with psychologist Bonnie Jacobson that "yelling is a gesture of impotence." It means you're not listening, and listening creates empathy, which can change behavior.

It is surprising how many people consider only two mind tracks, or solutions, to the important dilemmas in their lives. Their grave error is in using the past as a reference point. For example, just because a person had two divorces doesn't mean that a third marriage won't work. You have to create alternative reality with new positive thought forms. Visualize and affirm it and make it real. If old patterns arise, don't get discouraged. Realize that it's just a bad thinking habit you can change.

CLEAN UP RELATIONSHIPS DAILY

In one of my workshops, I recall a couple who had the following pattern: Dave would be angry with Janet for something but he wouldn't tell her. He would pretend to "get over it," but would be seething inside. Janet had the exact same tendency. She would never tell Dave what made her angry with him. They would both "stuff it." Then the pressure would build and build and finally they would have a knock-down drag-out fight and scream out all the complaints they had stored up. This was "dumping" on the highest order. They were always fighting about situations that happened two months ago, sometimes even a year ago. They were never in present time and one or the other would always deny what they said or did back then. Then they would get in a fight about a fight.

After the workshop, they literally started *all over*. They made a simple agreement to clean up their relationship every night or on the spot if possible, but at least every night. They both stuck to this agreement and it worked. Besides, they often found out that they weren't really upset with each other for the reasons they thought, and there wasn't much to fight about anymore. But when problems did come up, they would talk it out on the same day, and start each new day fresh as though they had a "new" relationship.

It is a good policy to have an agreement in your present relationship to clean up disputes at least every night. It is better to clean them up on the spot, but sometimes that isn't always appropriate. But if you want a light, joyful relationship, don't wait another day to communicate complaints.

Each night you can simply say to your roommate, lover, or spouse, "Is there anything you need to communicate to me before we go to sleep?" If you do this, then nothing builds up and each new day starts anew. Eventually this process will become integrated into your life as a good habit, and you won't even need to ask the question to remind each other.

The amount of love that flows between the two of you is often controlled by the quantity and quality of your communications. After you have cleaned up the day's withheld communications, complete the process by acknowledging yourself and your partner for successes. Then you can drop off to sleep in a happy state of mind or have sex without a lot of "psychic garbage" between you.

FIND THE HIGHEST SPIRITUAL THOUGHT

Many couples I've worked with argue because they each get stuck on their "position." He thinks for sure that he's right and she thinks for sure she's right. Neither will budge from their position as they continue to fight. This could go on for years. I assure you, there is another way to play the game and it's also exciting.

Marvin and Thelma were fighting about whether or not to move. Thelma said they had outgrown the house and there wasn't enough room anymore. She felt crowded and depressed; and besides the house was always damp and musty because of their location. This problem had gotten worse over the years; there was no way to get rid of the dampness. Marvin said they could never get another house for the same money and they couldn't afford anything else. They fought about this continually without a resolution. I told them it was time to *go for solution* and that there was a higher spiritual thought: That they could *both* win. This had never occurred to them for some reason.

I asked them to entertain the thought that they *could* find a house that was spacious, dry, and warm and at a price that was just as affordable. Or they could literally dispose of some of their "stuff" and find some way to clear up the dampness. Both thoughts were positive as opposed to the two negative positions that they had held. The first step was to move them off their negative positions. The next step was to find the highest thought that would allow them to each get what they wanted. They chose to move, because Marvin surrendered to a higher thought; he went from "It's impossible" to "It might be possible." They did in fact find a new house at a reasonable price.

It cost a little bit more, but because there was more room, Thelma was able to start her own mail order business at home, and they soon had more income plus a new house.

There is always another way where both of you can win.

Never allow yourself to stay stuck in any position. You can always feel out the highest thought by listening to your body. The highest thought is always the most positive, the least limiting, the most truthful, and the most productive. It "feels" the best in your body. This strategy prevents all power struggles and fights. It has been adopted by trainers and certified Rebirthers play it naturally.

When each person is always willing to surrender to the highest spiritual thought, this doesn't imply giving away power to another. With a couple, sometimes one partner may have the higher spiritual thought and sometimes the other. If my partner has it, I leave my position and rise to the level of the higher thought. If I have the higher thought, my partner does the same.

In business meetings or other group situations, when the highest thought has been presented and everyone recognizes it, then people stop being "stuck" and rise to the new level. Everyone is relieved and happy no matter who came up with the thought. When confusion arises as to which is the highest thought, meditate alone rather than fight it out.

Always look at your life to see what results you're creating and attracting. Consider what thoughts have produced these results. A crucial test is when your mate is reacting to you in some way that you don't approve. Look at yourself and see why you might be drawing that kind of behavior from your mate and why your subconscious desired that reaction. You must also take responsibility for attracting the kind of person who demonstrates that behavior.

Work on your own to upgrade the level of your thinking, and ask your partner to do the same. You will be amazed at the results.

Problem Solving

Do you remember the problem-solving dynamic that your family used when you were growing up? Who gave their power away to whom? Did your parents openly fight? Who usually won and how did he or she do this? Did the parent who was most angry force the other finally to cave in? Did that parent "stuff it all" and sulk? Did one parent storm out? Were conflicts actually resolved?

Think about your own problem-solving dynamics. Are you imitating your parents? What methods are *you* practicing?

Anger is hard on your body. The organs suffer and, what is known as the etheric body, takes a real beating. Anger also makes you age. During an argument, even when a very angry person "wins," she usually feels guilty afterwards, and the other is left withered and resentful. Either outcome drains us. Fighting is simply not an enlightened way of solving problems; it's a bad habit. Yet, perhaps because it is so commonplace, many still defend it, and there are many schools of thought that promote it.

People also have many excuses for defending and justifying anger. Often they righteously cling to it. *A Course in Miracles* states very clearly that anger can *never* be justified because *attack has no foundation* (Text, p. 593). The first obstacle to peace, it adds, is *the desire to get rid of [peace]* (Text, p. 380). In other words, the wish to be angry.

Although I've not always maintained the peace during every waking hour, this ideal *has* been and *remains* my goal. Since I committed myself to peace, I've only lived with men who share that ideal and are willing to stay with it. Of course, we are human beings, and temporary setbacks occur whenever we are processing the ego. These hitches, however, can be dealt with easily, once both parties agree that peace is their priority.

There are those who find peace boring and believe life would be terribly dull without the "drama" of troubled relationships. I must simply ask these people, "Are you willing to see this differently?" All we have to do is tune in to the *spirit* of peace, and all the glory of the Kingdom of Heaven opens to us. This joyous experience creates a passion so exhilarating that once you feel it, you'll never revert to conflictive behavior.

This spirit can only be felt when we rise above conflict and anger. For beneath every irritation, a well of hatred lies hidden. What's more, our job doesn't end with the elimination of external conflict and anger. We must deal firmly with internal conflict. In other words, we may not be openly fighting with our mate, but *in our own mind* we can still be in turmoil over them or with ourselves. Our own conflicting thoughts can keep us from finding peace, an attribute that we possess naturally.

Some people believe, in their struggle to be creative, that their trials and tribulations are necessary, if not desirable. They wrestle with the creative process and believe that hard times induce them to create. Little do they realize that they might produce even more beautiful and exciting works if they were free of constant struggle. The spirit of peace gives rise to tremendous creativity. It stimulates a natural, flowing creative process that requires no effort at all. When two people in a relationship simultaneously access this creative harmony, they experience an unimaginable thrill. This synergy is magical and produces a near sexual experience. What potential we have! Why waste time diluting it with conflict?

Yet we can only mine these natural resources under favorable circumstances. When two opposing thought systems collide, it becomes impossible to attain peace of mind or peace in your relationships. We must choose one or the other: either the Holy Spirit's thought system or the ego's. The ego's thought system—based on the idea that you are separate from God and all others—leads nowhere. It merely consists of a collection of all the negative thoughts we hold about life, ourselves, and other people. It leads us on a tour that passes from separation to fear, worry, depression, sickness, and death. As long as we indulge in such negative thinking and oppose the Holy Spirit's thought system, we confine ourselves to hell. Knowing we are one with God leads us to peace, abundance, health, and aliveness.

Because I knew there had to be a better alternative to arguing, I prayed for years for a way to prevent arguments. The simple technique which finally came to me allows us to turn matters over to the Holy Spirit.

Before starting the game, each person reviews aloud how he's handled conflicts in the past. Did the method of conflict resolution work? Or did it end with one person manipulating the other? Did "resolution" mean that the "angriest" one took over, controlling and beating the other down emotionally? Did it amount to fighting over the issue until both people were exhausted? None of these methods bring satisfaction. They're destructive. We must be willing to look at the habits we've developed in the course of our relationships. Addiction to the old ways will prevent one from trying the new ones. After each person has evaluated the past, he or she must recognize the failure of old methods and agree to release them. In this way, a space of openness is created, and new conflict resolution methods can arise.

Are you willing to find a better solution to problems than simply fighting?

I want to make it clear that I am *not* advising you to avoid expressing your feelings, for suppression is also very destructive to the body. Unpleasant feelings can tie you up in knots and cause disease; expressing these emotions diminishes their power over you. But expression is not an end in itself; the goal is to air your feelings and *release them*.

You can express your emotions without having screaming fits or huge, destructive fights. You can let your feelings be known in a way that is not harmful to you or others. Beginning with the words "I feel upset right now" works for me. After that, if I share all of my feelings, my discomfort can fade away. Because I use this technique, I know that I can create the space for someone to listen to me. I don't have to blow up. If the conflict centers on a very charged issue, I lie down and breathe out the emotions. Spiritual purification techniques show us that we can solve conflicts gently; we don't need to explode. This is why rebirthing is so effective.

In addition, once we realize that our disturbing feelings result from negative thinking, we have the power to transform those feelings by changing our thoughts. Expressing yourself fully must become a way of life. You have a right to express *all* of your feelings; when you value yourself, you realize that. The techniques that you find most useful are also those that benefit you most.

I am well aware that a number of contemporary self-help books actually *encourage* us to fight; I recently came across a guide whose author asserts that those who don't fight simply don't care about life! Such books not only advocate fighting, they also provide directions about how to fight "well." Within this context, it is certainly true that not everyone in the world has learned how to deal with anger and *if* you *are* going to fight, you should not name-call and be abusive. Try a completely different tactic—making it your goal to *give up* anger instead of cultivating it. If you feel angry, why not work it out in ways other than yelling at your mate or family members? You can run around the block, scream in the shower or when driving alone in your car. I recommend lying down and breathing out your tension and emotions on the exhales. Kicking our legs scissors style while breathing and keeping our knees straight can also lessen tension. Perhaps you have developed other techniques that help you cope with anger in a positive way.

Comic behavior is another way of keeping an argument from building or stopping one. Did you know that some police officers are even taught to use comedy in their work? During their training, officers are sometimes taught to end domestic fights by acting in an unexpected or humorous manner. For instance, they may walk over to the refrigerator and help themselves to sandwich fixings! Seeing one of them acting so casually can be such a shock to the battling partners that they often stop fighting right then and there. Our minds can create a myriad of helpful tools to diminish our rage. But the fundamental discipline we must master is to release the negative thoughts that cause the anger. When you change these, anger will dissolve entirely.

People other than self-help authors promote fighting as a helpful tool: even therapists have vehemently disagreed with me about the importance of releasing anger. Sadly, some of them have wanted to fight with me about the issue of fighting! One in particular—a highly trained therapist from Switzerland—once gave me a long lecture defending anger. I let him express his opinion and decided to wait until after he attended our spiritual retreat to discuss the issue further. At the retreat, we all studied *A Course in Miracles* together, dividing the text in sections and teaching them to each other. As fate would have it, he happened to get a lesson that focused precisely on the subject of anger! He studied it with sincerity, and in the end, I didn't have to explain anything further. As his turn to speak arrived, he stood up in front of all the students, declaring humbly, "All my life I have defended anger. Now after reading this *Course*, I see that I was wrong." Shortly afterward he met and fell in love with his true soul mate. Over the years, he has gone on to defend peace, both personally and within his professional practice, based on that lesson he learned from the *Course:*

> Anger always involves projection of separation, which must ultimately be accepted as one's own responsibility, rather than being blamed on others. Anger cannot occur unless you believe that you have been attacked and that attack is justified in return, and that you are in no way responsible for it. Given these wholly irrational premises, the equally irrational conclusion that a brother is worthy of

attack rather than love must follow. You cannot be attacked, attack has no justification and you are responsible for what you believe. (Text, p. 84)

Let's further explore just what occurs when we allow anger to overcome us. Psychologist Bonnie Jacobson has said that "yelling is a gesture of impotence." Among adults it causes rifts because it means you're not listening. Listening creates empathy, and empathy can create changes in behavior.

If you're intent on making these changes, Jacobson suggests that you first observe how you tense up when your mate says something that bothers you. After that, take a breath and "shelve" your anger for five minutes. The most important part of this process is to ask your partner questions about his angry statement so you can follow his line of reasoning. If, for example, he says, "I wish you didn't spend so much time with that friend of yours!" don't snap back. Try asking questions: "Oh, don't you like her?" Keep asking questions until something opens up. Try using your intuition to find out what really lies behind this statement. For example, you might inquire, "Do you feel I spend too little time with you?" Even if the answer is no, he'll appreciate your concern. Tell him how you heard his statement, what you thought it meant. This way he can correct or confirm your understanding.

Let me say it once more: *keep listening and asking questions*. If you're addicted or just accustomed to anger, you may forget this infinitely important principle. And you must discipline yourself. You must also continually ask yourself, "Do I *really* want peace?"

In his book *Peace, Love and Healing*, cancer surgeon Bernie Siegal provides a list of the "symptoms of inner peace," composed by chiropractor Jeff Rockwell and his wife. With prolonged exposure, any one of us can eventually exhibit these "symptoms."

THE SYMPTOMS OF INNER PEACE

1. A tendency to think and act spontaneously rather than from fears based on past experiences.
2. An unmistakable ability to enjoy each moment.
3. A loss of interest in judging one's self.
4. A loss of interest in judging others.
5. A loss of interest in conflict.
6. A loss of interest in interpreting the actions of others.
7. A loss of ability to worry (this is a very serious symptom).
8. Frequent, overwhelming episodes of appreciation.
9. Contented feelings of connectedness with others and nature.
10. Frequent attacks of smiling through the eyes of the heart.
11. Increasing susceptibility to love extended by others as well as the uncontrollable urge to extend it.
12. An increasing tendency to let things happen rather than to make them happen.

If you have all or even most of the above symptoms, please be advised that your condition of peace may be so far advanced as to not be treatable.

MIND TRACKS

It's surprising to find that many people consider only two mind tracks, or solutions, to the important dilemmas in their lives—and both of these options lead nowhere. For instance, a married woman who has felt stifled in her marriage for years may think along these lines:

If I stay in this relationship, I will never be able to be myself and do what I want to do, but *if I leave this relationship, I will not find anyone else and will be alone forever.*

A single man deliberating on whether to make a commitment to a problematic partnership may limit himself this way:

If I get committed to this relationship, then she might leave me and the pain of abandonment would be too much to bear, but *if she doesn't leave me, then I would have to stay in the relationship and put up with all her bullshit.*

Or there is the case of a dissatisfied employee, which highlights a common professional quandary:

If I stay in this career, then I'll never get to do what I really want, but *if I leave this career I won't have enough money to pursue anything else.*

Many clients come to see me believing that these diametrically opposed alternatives are actually their *only* options. Their grave error lies in using the past as a reference point. Just because relationships have gone one way in the past *does not mean* that they have to turn out that way in the future. For example, just because a person had two divorces *does not* mean that the third marriage won't work. Likewise, just because a person has committed to unsatisfying relationships in the past *does not* mean all future commitments will be unsatisfying. Watch out for the tendency to become stuck on mind tracks that go nowhere, or to reinforce those tracks, adding to their effect.

When I help my clients create an alternative reality, I often suggest that they imagine the existence of a *new* railway system. The old tracks veer off to the sides, and the trains that travel along them carry the obsolete thought patterns. They've been officially condemned because they're antiquated and potentially dangerous to the health. What we need are brand new cars on a new track carrying fresh ideas.

An example of a "new track" would be something like this:

I can stay in a relationship and be myself, or *I can leave and find others that are even better.*

At first the new track will feel strange or unfamiliar because the engineer is accustomed to the old track—the old thought pattern. That is exactly why it helps to picture a new track and to begin reinforcing the new reality. You have to convince yourself that you can build this new reality by visualizing it, affirming it, and making it real. First, you must realize that you're addicted to the old thought patterns. Begin to see the old tracks as boring, notice that they are actually repellent. Feel the excitement of the new track—and then add the final ingredient—faith. Faith is extremely important.

Even when you find yourself moving down the same old tracks, don't get discouraged. Realize that it's just a habit. Think what it's like to be an American in England, where the driver's seat is on the opposite side of the car. At first, you keep entering the car on the wrong side. This is a habit deeply ingrained from the age of 16. Then one day, after weeks of making the same mistake, you remember to get in on the right side. You've corrected the behavior that doesn't serve you. You have broken the habit.

Through counseling, I've known a number of people, both as single individuals and then afterwards as part of a couple. It has been interesting to compare how different people fared in these two situations. Some became stronger, healthier, and *more* powerful as part of a couple. Many, however, became weaker: these people actually lost self-esteem, and the partners eventually caved in on themselves.

Determining why one couple grows while another couple self-destructs can be a very complicated undertaking. Indeed, so many factors contribute to the relationship's strength or weakness that it may be impossible to say exactly which factors cause a particular outcome. Certain harmful tendencies are fairly easy to identify, if one is trained to observe behavior in relationships. When you end up weaker instead of stronger in a relationship, some of these types of destructive behavior are usually in evidence:

- Making the relationship top priority over everything else—neglecting the other parts of life.
- Making your mate more important than God, yourself, and everyone else. Idolizing or worshipping this person to the detriment of your own self-esteem.

- Assigning the relationship over to a priority other than spirituality.
- Attempting to become *just like* your mate and losing your individuality in the process.
- Being afraid to communicate your own ideas.
- Being afraid to confront your mate on weak areas and "stuffing" resentment about those areas.
- Protecting one's mate from productive criticism or feedback from others.
- Becoming insular, not having enough exposure to new friends and creative outlets. Getting into ruts.
- Giving your personal power away to the mate.
- The tendency for each partner to assume a set "role."
- Sinking into old family patterns.
- Lacking self-esteem.

As these habits increasingly erode each partner's self-esteem, the tendencies themselves get stronger and stronger, and the couple becomes *stuck*. This dynamic makes it difficult to stop the destruction. Radical measures aimed at recapturing each individual's health and self-respect may be in order.

How will you know if you've found a solid, positive relationship? It won't be hard to tell. A negative, unholy relationship feels depleting, like a depressing burden. But a healthy, holy relationship is entirely different. It nourishes each mate's individuality, strength, power, creativity, and productivity in the world. Each partner has a personal spiritual life and considers their spirituality the top priority—the relationship comes second. There is a spontaneity and moment-by-moment flow between real human beings rather than rigid role playing by two-dimensional caricatures. Each partner feels safe to give the other constructive feedback that produces *movement*— within the relationship there is no fear of communicating *anything*. Each person easily maintains a high degree of self-esteem because both partners are constantly centered in spirituality. Each partner supports the other's "coming out" and getting into power and is not threatened or jealous of these efforts. Each knows how to process family patterns that come up without getting stuck. The techniques the two have created for clearing problems work because everything they do is *life-supporting*, and synergy and harmony abound.

RELATIONSHIP DYNAMICS

CHAPTER 5

When it comes to communicating with others, the key factor is not only your innate communication skills but how well you know yourself. Good communication is a natural expression of your divinity. While early family dynamics can impede that connection and make clear communications difficult, you have to find the path back to yourself. This is your truth, and I've found that "telling the truth faster is more fun per hour."

When this misperception persists, it can lead to what I call the yes-no problem. You say you want one thing, but your behavior creates just the opposite outcome. These "mixed" messages create confusion and make you angry because your partner isn't responding as expected. You need to know who you really are to know what you really want and to communicate it clearly.

Acting from a state of limitation creates these kinds of blocks. I've found that having an attitude of Love, Praise, and Gratitude will attract all that you want in life, including wonderful friends and mates. The Source thrives on having you receive from it, because the giver always expands by giving. So don't block the things you deserve to receive, and don't block the love that is there for you.

This will only happen when you stop fighting with yourself and others. Often this is behavior carried over from childhood when we either conformed or rebelled against our parents' wishes. And if you've set your mate up as one of your parents, you may then end up unconsciously conforming with or rebelling against them. Either way, your behavior is reactive. Take a good look at your relationship. Are these forces at play? If so, take responsibility and change them.

It is important for couples to establish methods and rules for solving such problems. Two of the most helpful problem-solving processes are: Creating the right state of mind and learning how to be an active listener. Remember that you and your mate are on the same side, are trying to create solutions and not just win, and that you can disagree without upsetting each other. Try sitting down across from each other and really listening to what the other has to say. It's important that all sharing be done without blame.

THE ILLUSION OF EGO

The source of most human conflict, according to *A Course in Miracles*, is misperceiving ourselves, our brothers, even God, as strangers that we then attack. You were made in the image of God, but you mistakenly think that you're separate. This separate self, your ego, isn't real. Only your perfection is real. *Thus, your brother is like you. Your sister is like you.* The only conflict is with yourself.

Let's begin, then, to know ourselves, to get clear on who we are. This beautiful passage in *A Course in Miracles* can be the starting point.

> WHAT AM I
> I am God's Son, complete and healed and whole, shining in the reflection of His love. In me is His creation sanctified and guaranteed eternal life. In me is love perfected, fear impossible, and joy established without opposite. I am the holy home of God Himself. I am the Heaven where His love resides. I am His holy Sinlessness Itself, for in my purity abides His Own (Workbook, p. 469).

This is your *true reality*. Nothing else is real. You were made in the image of God. You were made perfect. Perfection is your reality. You mistakenly think you can make imperfect what was made perfect. You made the mistake of thinking you were separate from God, and then you made up your own separate self which is not real, because it is impossible to be separate from God. Therefore your ego, which is the separated self, is not real. Only your perfection is real.

Your brother is like you. Your sister is like you. All of humanity is like you. See in your sisters and brothers (mates) God's creation. He or she is a mirror of your self.

1. Would it be possible for you to hate your brother if you were like him?
2. Could you attack him if you realized you journey with him toward the same goal?
3. Wouldn't you help him reach it in every way you could, if his attainment of it were perceived as yours?

Your brother is your friend because his Father created him like you. There is no difference (paraphrase, Text, pp. 465–466).

The *Course* forewarns us that we may oppose its teachings precisely because they reveal that each of us is like all others. There can never be true harmony among those who are different, for the pursuit of specialness will always bring pain (paraphrase, Text, pp. 466–467).

You must perceive your brother only as you see him now. Find the present. His past has no reality in the present. See him without his past. Perceive him as born again. His errors are all past, and by perceiving him without them, you are releasing him—and yourself.

See the Holy Spirit in your brother. See his innocence. See his perfection. The present offers your brothers in a light you can share with them—and in so doing, you free your past. Would you then hold the past against them? If you do, you are choosing to remain in darkness (paraphrase, Text, p. 233).

COMMUNICATION

The ability to communicate well often seems like an innate talent some of us have and some of us don't, or it's a simple matter of timing and good techniques. These factors certainly facilitate communication, but others—especially self-knowledge and high self-esteem—play an equally important role. When you are more certain of who you are, and see yourself as an equal, communication with others improves a great deal. You're no longer afraid to express yourself or to speak up and ask for what you want. You are neither quiet or loud, nor hesitant or pushy. You are spontaneous and your words come out just right. Good communication has become a natural expression of your divinity.

If you're having trouble communicating, you need to discover the source of the problem. Why do you have this communication block? What is the negative thought behind it?

If you grew up in a household where parents gave each other the silent treatment, where one family member dominated everything with his or her communication, where people were afraid to express what they felt, or where it wasn't safe to tell the truth, you were given a model that actually *impeded* rather than promoted clear communications. You will have to undo the damage. You *can* and you *should*. There is absolutely no need to spend your whole life communicating poorly just because your family did. You may have learned their habits, but you can *unlearn* them, too.

Because I was verbally abused for saying the truth to my father as a child, I was afraid of telling the total truth to men I loved. I would always say just what I thought men wanted to hear. Ultimately, I ended up going into therapy over this reluctance. Through practice, I overcame my block against telling the truth, and now I *always* say what I feel—and people, including men, always know how I feel. They like it and I like it. It feels good. The truth works.

"Tell the complete truth faster and there is more fun per hour." In other words, the sooner you tell the truth, the more you'll enjoy life. Here is a simple exercise in telling the truth: You let your mate tell you all their feelings on a subject for fifteen minutes straight. You listen without interrupting. Then you repeat what you thought they said. Now switch roles and begin the exercise again. This feedback technique will help you see how well you're listening and communicating.

Here is another learning exercise: You tell your mate, "Something I saw as a child but felt I could not communicate was _____," or "Something I feel I can't communicate now is _____," filling in the blanks. If too much fear comes up, say, "The reasons I'm afraid to communicate this are _____," completing the sentence with clear-sighted and honest reflections. Notice how you feel about yourself and your partner before and afterwards.

What do you notice about the two processes above? What tone do these particular questions set? If you use these techniques, you'll soon recognize what a difference politeness, respect, and clear boundaries make! An open mind, willing to accept and acknowledge a partner's efforts and willingness to change, actually facilitate those shifts in behavior! Telling the truth faster doesn't imply the sacrifice of graciousness. Relentless nagging can only spoil progress. There are much more effective means than nagging.

Stop and ask yourself why you're saying something in a way that the other person can't hear. The way to be heard is to say what you have to say without blame. Once someone perceives blame in what you're saying, their options are to blame back, or tune you out. For instance, if you accuse your partner of never helping with the dishes, the implication is that they're a bad person; they've failed in some way. Instead, if you explain that you're tired by the end of the week and need help around the house, you'd be much more likely to get it. If your partner is doing the nagging, choose to hear it not as blame, but simply as information. For instance, if they accuse you of not picking up after yourself, you can thank them for the reminder. If you find yourself actually picking a fight, this may be a cover for a deeper problem. If your partner wants to have sex and you don't, they may not complain at the time. However, in the morning, they may find fault with something as trivial as the way you prepared breakfast. If a fight ensues, rest assured it has little to do with breakfast and more to do with releasing tension and anger, consequently circumventing the real issue: rejection. Nagging won't reveal the true issue at hand. Patience and understanding will.

Double Messages: The Yes-No Problem

Just what are double messages? They happen all the time. A person may say, "I really want you to be with me," while conveying "Don't get close to me" in the same breath.

- "I really love you but I really hate you."
- "I really want a relationship that works but nothing you do is right."
- "I really want to succeed but don't make me come out of the womb."
- "I really want you to make a lot of money, but I wish you'd stop working so hard and abandoning me."

By paying close attention, we can often discover a whole range of such examples in our own lives. We claim to want one thing, but our behavior creates just the opposite outcome. These "mixed" messages confuse others and make us angry because we aren't getting what we want in our relationships. This continuous cycle of double messages and frustration will leave your body a wreck.

If giving double messages describes the modus operandi of you or your partner, you may also feel discouraged about clearing up anything in your relationship. This is near impossible when one or both partners don't see that they're sending double messages to each other, and sometimes even to themselves. Let me illustrate what I mean. A person who conveys the message, "I want to have sex with you," and then doesn't allow lovemaking to follow has traditionally been labeled a "tease," and we generally look upon them with disdain. But simple condemnation prevents us from asking the deeper question: why might someone act that way? Perhaps they want to get even with the opposite sex. Or maybe they're too scared to come into intimate contact with a real person, or don't think they deserve pleasure—perhaps their feigned seductiveness stems from a combination of these factors.

Although we often associate double messages with sexual interactions, they actually come up all the time in different areas of life. Whether it's around sex, children, commitment, or power relations, yes-no energy *always* reveals unresolved conflict and a lack of self-knowledge. To avoid this set-up, you not only have to know what you want, you have to communicate it clearly, and make sure your message is free of counterintentions.

Let's say your partner tells you they want peace—but subconsciously they believe, "I need anger in order to survive," or "Anger makes me feel powerful." No technique would effectively bring them tranquility because their underlying thoughts would sabotage peace. As long as their subconscious beliefs go unchallenged, they'll have the tendency to unconsciously set up conflicts and manipulate events to have an excuse to get angry. This person doesn't really want peace, they would rather be angry. They may insist, "But I do want peace. I just can't contain my anger." Using a lack of control as an excuse and anger as a sort of addiction is no answer. Their only addiction, in this case, is their refusal to get clear.

One of the most difficult jobs we have in life is to look deeply within ourselves, acknowledging, along with our nobler feelings, our errors, pettiness, and lack of love. It isn't easy to admit we may be giving others double messages. But if you're frustrating and hurting people around you in this way, take responsibility for it. Ambivalence that stems from laziness creates a *no-win* situation. And if you are the one being jerked around in this way, you must also take responsibility for it. Why do you need to be treated in this way? Why should you participate in a no-win situation?

When we're clear, our actions match our words. We neither convey mixed messages, nor harbor "hidden agendas." It becomes easy for others to give us what we ask for because the request has been openly communicated. When we have these good feelings, we've conquered the rule of the ego. Clarity, in the mind of the Holy Spirit, is just that: clear, easy, smooth, rewarding, satisfying energy.

HAVE THE RIGHT ATTITUDE

A wonderful little book, *The Door of Everything*, channeled by Ruby Nelson, outlines the "Ascension" attitudes. Adopting these attitudes will bring you good relationships, and they will also thrust you into an altogether fabulous life. The Ascension attitudes are Love, Praise, and Gratitude. If your being radiates these attitudes, you'll easily attract all the wonderful friends and mates you could ever want.

Giving thanks for the good things you have always brings you more. Many people focus on what they don't have, and when I've done this for any length of time, it has led me into misery. Catherine Ponder, in discussing the principle of giving thanks, says that your highest good is there for you, even if you aren't experiencing it yet. Give thanks that your perfect mate is out there in the universe and admit that you've not been ready to receive. God is ready when you are.

The Source thrives on having you receive from it, because the giver always expands by the giving. So don't block the things you deserve to receive, and don't block the love that is there for you. In the same way, if you lose something, know that it was no longer best for you, and that the Source is clearing the way to give you something even greater.

If you focus on loss, you'll get more loss. If you give thanks for what you have, you'll get more.

I've always tried to have the attitude that whatever happens is the perfect thing at that time. Even if it seems "bad" at first, I always know that it probably happened so I could get the lesson. I always manage to turn everything into a "win." With this attitude, I never lose and I stay happy.

CONFORMING AND REBELLING

Day in and day out, do you tend to rebel or conform—or have you transcended those tendencies and become your own self? How about your mate—is she or he a conformist or a rebel? This is good to know. During childhood, we generally conform to our parent's wishes or rebel against them. We may be doing some of both, but usually one pattern is stronger. While these behavior patterns are normal in childhood and adolescence, they don't serve us well in our adult lives. We must either face and resolve this childhood-based tendency or risk causing perpetual conflict in our adult relationships.

If you've set up your mate as one of your parents, you then may end up doing nearly everything they say (conforming) or doing everything in opposition to their wishes (rebelling). Either way, your behavior is reactive. You're not responding in the *present*. You're still in the past. If your mate might suggest something and you tend to conform, you may do it even if you don't really like the idea, and even if it's not actually good for you. And later, there is a good chance you will resent it. If you're the rebel, on the other hand, you may very likely refuse something perfectly reasonable even though it might be a lot of fun. Again, you both lose out.

Go back in your mind and review your childhood history. What was your role in the family? If family members were to label you either a conformer or a rebel, which term would they use?

Now consider your past relations. Did your "knee-jerk" rebelliousness cause conflict where none existed? Did it make a relatively fair partner someone you had to fight against? Or was your tendency to conform, letting yourself be manipulated until your partner lost respect for you—or until you lost your sense of self? More importantly, take a good look at your current relationship. What forces are at play now? Have you processed your childhood tendencies to conform or rebel? These may be your issues—sometimes you'll have to process them away from your mate. If these old tendencies still influence your behavior, take responsibility for them and work to change them.

Problem Solving in the New Paradigm

In the New Paradigm, a person who is committed to truth believes in telling the complete truth *faster* (and has more fun as a result). It's important for couples to establish methods and rules for problem solving, methods that you both like and can honor. It's important that you agree to reserve the right to remind your partner of these methods. Two of the most helpful problem-solving processes are: Creating the right state of mind and learning how to be an active listener.

STATE OF MIND

1. Remember that you and your mate, or partner in business, are on the same side wanting to solve the problem together.
2. Remember that the goal is to create a solution, not to drag out a debate where someone wins and someone loses.
3. Remember that you can disagree without upsetting each other.
4. Remember that there is a way to prevent arguments, but you both have to be willing to go for the highest spiritual thought.
5. Remember that using anger (as a way of manipulating, controlling, or getting what you want) isn't enlightened. The goal is always to be as enlightened as possible.

6. To get what you want, you have to ask for it. If the other person doesn't want what you want, then you have the choice of negotiating a compromise until each sees the intrinsic value of the solution, together or separately.

7. Find out which points you can agree on and acknowledge those which help you relax, such as, "I agree that you deserve to have more time to yourself . . . but how can we also get enough time for the children?"

ACTIVE LISTENING

1. Sit down and face each other and look into each other's eyes. One of you begins to share and the other simply listens without interruption. A timer can be used so that each person has ten minutes or so to talk uninterrupted. If you're the listener, you should *not* be rehearsing what you are going to say. In fact, you should listen well enough that you can actually report back what has been said: You might say, "The main thing I think you're saying to me is that you really feel hurt by what I did at the party last night." The listener doesn't defend or explain anything. You only summarize what you heard to make sure your understanding is accurate.

2. If you're the person communicating and feel that the listener didn't understand something, then you must repeat it until it can be repeated back. Good communication is the responsibility of the communicator.

3. *Listen* to what is said. Ask yourself what it is you need or want to hear. Learn about where you need to improve your listening habits.
4. When the communicator feels that he or she was actually heard properly, then you can switch roles.

It's important to remember that all sharing should be done without blame. Also, each party must be willing to look at how they've helped to create the upset. This is a key point in an enlightened paradigm. When both people take responsibility, nothing happens!

My Australian acupuncturist, Vicki Wooler, has this sign on her wall:

IS THIS A PROBLEM OR AN OPPORTUNITY TO LEARN?

RELATIONSHIP CLEARING

CHAPTER 6

When relationships get stuck, the first step is realizing that you've reached an impasse. This sounds deceptively easy, but many of us are in denial about this basic problem. At this point, the situation calls for spiritual purification: rebirthing, chanting, or reading *A Course in Miracles*. Of course, continual purification can prevent the problem from arising in the first place.

One symptom of a "stuck" relationship is constantly and often unfairly finding fault with your mate. You may be projecting, and your mate may unconsciously act out your projection, or since you've actually come to expect it, you may even "draw" it out of them. In any case, you need to take 100 percent responsibility for *everything* that happens in your life. That's the first step to clearing it.

Guilt very often "runs" or controls such relationships. You have to work it out to allow yourself all the pleasure that comes with a perfect relationship. If you feel guilty about something, you know that forgiveness is lacking. You can start by forgiving yourself for any failure or transgression. Forgiveness is the path for the return to innocence—the natural human state of unconditional love, satisfaction, peace, and power.

In any relationship, difficulties or conflicts will come up. The old way of dealing with conflict was to find something wrong with the other person, to make that person wrong. The enlightened way is to process yourself and each other. Both partners need to clear their issues with the support of their mate. At the same time, avoid overprocessing, or your relationship will resemble an endless therapy session.

You must treat dysfunction in a relationship like a physical illness and treat it immediately. If you don't deal with a problem right away, your anger becomes suppressed, tension builds, and your relationship becomes unhealthy. By the time you get emergency help, it may be too late. And processing doesn't have to be hard work. It can be fun, a practical new way of living in which you're clearing your relationship and your body moment by moment.

Ideally, you will treat all your relationships, from partners to friendships, in this manner, and clear them at the end of each encounter. Developing the habit of getting clear on the spot will prove extremely beneficial to your health, self-esteem, and peace of mind. Though you may feel awkward at first, after a while clearing becomes more and more natural. Remember, when clearing be honest. *Don't* agree with people just to make temporary peace. You will resent having "given in," and this will harm the relationship.

GETTING YOURSELF UNSTUCK

In working toward righting a relationship, you must first learn how to get yourself "unstuck." The first step—realizing that you have reached an impasse—sounds deceptively easy. The truth is that many of us are in denial about this basic problem. Because we often won't admit that we have problems at all, I've listed seven signs that will help you recognize when you're stuck:

- You feel unhappy and isolated.
- You feel anxious or moody, rarely experiencing joy.
- You feel helpless, can't move forward, or accomplish ordinary projects and activities.
- You are sick, in pain, as if your vital energy is blocked.
- You feel a nagging urge to attack someone verbally or physically.
- You can't get your personal relationship to clear.
- Your financial situation is shaky or faltering.

If you've experienced any of these difficulties, you'll need to give yourself some special attention. The situation calls for a spiritual purification. Rebirthing, chanting, reading *A Course in Miracles*, and prayer are the ones I use most frequently. If you're unable to use any of these techniques, you can write down your negative thoughts on a piece of paper and change them to affirmations. This will at least give you some immediate relief.

Another writing technique I use for clearing is to compose a letter to God and place it on my altar. In the message, I bare my soul, but I don't plead to God to take my problems away. Instead, you should *confess* your case, describing your negative thoughts and addictions to those thoughts. Offer your words up to the Holy Spirit, Jesus, Babaji, or whatever works for you. Decide that you will think differently, and ask God to strengthen your new thoughts with energy. This technique always works for me. I have written to my Master, Babaji, in this way for years and, afterwards, I usually release my anxiety by crying. Then, if I've been stuck, I can let go and trust again.

Of course, preventing problems is the best policy to pursue. Spiritual purification keeps us from getting stuck. But during times when we feel at a complete impasse, so stuck that we don't even feel like breathing, when we may not feel like praying, writing, or chanting—this is what I recommend: get your tape recorder and earphones, put on some chanting tapes with mantras such as *Om Namaha Shivaia*, and turn the volume way up. Lie down in front of your altar and relax until you break through the impasse. Take some deep breaths and let yourself cry. *It works.*

Taking Responsibility

When you love your mate, but still notice yourself constantly and often unfairly finding fault with her or him, there may be more to the matter than meets the eye. Frequently, when you find something wrong with your mate, you're actually seeing your partner as your mother, your father, or someone else in your past. Your mate then actually *becomes* that person to you, because you make them into that person unconsciously. This is a very common phenomenon; it is known as *projecting*. Because it is unconscious behavior, it may be difficult to catch yourself doing it—but it's valuable to at least be aware that you are projecting.

Sometimes, because of your projections, you misinterpret your partner's behavior. Other times your mate may unconsciously act out that behavior in your presence. Because you're familiar with such behavior, you've actually come to expect it and may even "draw it out" of another person! Your mate may, in fact, start behaving like someone in your past *for* you.

In any case, your job is to take 100 percent responsibility for *everything* that happens in your space. If your relationship is off-kilter, what is your part in it? What is your case? If your relationship is stuck, you can be certain that both of you are caught in a pattern. Blame becomes a useless distraction. If you get caught in blame, you cheat yourself of the opportunity to become more enlightened. Sometimes it may look as if the problem is entirely related to your partner's case and not your own. Don't be fooled! Ask yourself, "Why do I need that kind of behavior in my space? What is my payoff?" When we take total responsibility, the truth that is revealed can be very interesting.

When couples are stuck, I recommend a marriage counseling technique that is especially effective. The process has two parts. You begin by sitting across from your mate and saying, "What really upsets me about you is _____," or "What really bothers me about you is _____," and then completing the sentence. The second part of the exercise begins with, "Something I really appreciate about you is _____." You then complete the sentence with *the very same answers* you gave earlier. The idea, of course, is for you to realize that for some reason, you in fact *wanted* these challenges in your life, perhaps to complete some lesson, become aware of some pattern, or satisfy some need. The exercise ends with both partners thanking each other for being there to reveal their patterns. Your mate really is your guru!

GIVE UP GUILT

Guilt often controls relationships. This includes your relationship with money! Guilt is a symptom (much in the same way that fever is a symptom) that something is out of kilter in your relationship with the universe. If you're clear that you are a perfect manifestation of the Source, then guilt makes no sense. Guilt arises when we let ourselves forget our own divinity. Christians have identified sin as separation from God. *A Course in Miracles* states, "The continuing decision to remain separated is the only possible reason for continuing guilt feelings."

Many people go along letting their relationships work well and giving themselves a lot of pleasure until they suddenly reach their pleasure tolerance. This is an artificial barrier they've set up for themselves, which is controlled by guilt. The minute they start feeling guilty for having a wonderful relationship or for having an abundance of money, they'll begin fouling it up.

You have to work out guilt to believe you deserve a good relationship. You have to work out guilt to allow yourself all the pleasure that comes with a perfect relationship. And you have to work out guilt to handle money successfully.

You can start by forgiving yourself for any failure or transgressions you think you've made. Meditate on the thought: *I am innocent. My innocence brings peace, love, and abundance to me.*

Forgiveness is the path for the return to innocence—the return to the natural human state of unconditional love, satisfaction, peace, and power. Forgiveness is letting go of thoughts of revenge or retribution. Forgiveness is emotional disarmament.

Forgiveness is very simple. If you feel guilty about something, you know that forgiveness is lacking. Forgiveness has nothing to do with anyone but you. When you forgive someone, you may notice that they feel better about you, but that isn't the point. Forgiveness is about *you* feeling better about yourself. So, just as guilt is its own punishment, forgiveness is its own reward.

Jesus said, when asked how many times someone should forgive, "Seventy times seven." An effective way to practice this idea is to write forgiveness affirmations seventy times per day for a week. Guilt is all you have to lose by doing this.

Basic Forgiveness Affirmations

1. I forgive myself for hurting others.
2. I forgive others for hurting me.
3. I forgive myself for letting others hurt me.
4. I forgive others for letting me hurt them.

Assisting in the Clearing Process

Until we are all spiritual masters and are constantly holy, we will have baggage to clear. Thus, in any relationship, difficulties or conflicts will come up that need to be processed. The way in which we do this can make or break a positive relationship.

The old, unenlightened way of dealing with conflicts was to find something wrong with the other person, to pick on them, to point out faults continually; in other words, to make the other person wrong. As you may well know, this route leads nowhere.

If both you and your partner are on the path of enlightenment, however, and equally involved in spiritual purification to clear yourselves, processing can even be enjoyable. You can make helping each other clear into a game. At the same time, you must avoid the mistake of "over-processing" your mate. Otherwise, your relationship may come to resemble a continuous therapy session, which isn't the proper purpose of your union.

When the clearing process involves two partners, it should be based on certain agreements—a sort of "protocol." The partner who needs clearing can ask for the support of their mate or the person who is clearer at the time can offer their help. Never process someone without their permission—a person has to *want* to release it on their own. Even if you have the answer to your partner's problems, your truth will have no effect if they're not open to hearing it. As a partner, your job is to let them clear themselves in your presence by being there for them and by offering them a higher thought when they're ready. They may happen upon the higher thought by themselves. Or you can listen and ask questions until they discover it.

During a session, if my client is stuck in a great deal of pain and misery and wants assistance, I begin by finding out if they're willing to uncover the thought that is causing their misery. I am careful of my tone, so that they don't feel I'm making them wrong for having a negative thought. I want them to know I'm not trying to change them—the person they really are. I'm merely available to help them let go of destructive thoughts *if* and only *if* they feel ready. After establishing that my client is willing to search deeply, I might serve them by asking, "What negative thought is causing this pain?" Such a question often helps locate the deeply buried thought. In answering my question and verbalizing their thoughts, my client begins to release their emotions.

If you consistently find that your mate doesn't want to examine any of their thoughts, you'll have to suggest they find their own methods for clearing. If they refuse to clear themselves *at all*, then the relationship could prove very difficult in the long run. For a relationship to succeed, both parties really have to be willing to confront problems. If your mate isn't at all willing, then you must ask yourself the following questions:

■ What is my payoff for being with someone who is not willing to clear?

- How does this situation mirror my past?
- Am I using this person to hold me back?
- Before giving up, have I considered that he or she may be truly terrified? Does he or she perhaps need support in the area of fear?

To prevent the habit of "over-processing" each other, it is a good idea for each of you to have your own private rebirther. In an ideal arrangement, you would get rebirthed once every week or two by a trained rebirther, and then come back and share your experience in a light way with your mate. You might ask your partner to support you in further releasing those blocks by seeing you as healed.

Supporting someone who wants to clear themselves can be magic when the following ingredients are present:

- Your friend expressly asks for support from you.
- You give them total attention in a nurturing environment. You're not distracted.
- You have an attitude of love and acceptance and compassion. You listen. You're careful not to make judgments or put out negative energy.
- You have permission to ask them questions, and word them so as to help your friend discover their own answers.
- You hold the belief that they are perfect and healed and can overcome this.
- You get permission to offer them a higher thought if appropriate, but first create the space so that they may discover it themselves.

■ You thank them for the opportunity to serve, and you continue to hold the highest thoughts possible for them after you part.

This process can be relatively problem-free if you're helping someone with troubles that don't involve you. If you yourself are personally involved, you can still go ahead and use the same process. But you must be willing to have them do the same clearing on you. In other words, you must also be willing to honestly look at *your own part* in the problem. If the atmosphere is too charged with tension, however, and you're unable to work together in a supportive way, you should agree to get a third party who is skilled at assisting in clearing and not emotionally involved in the problem.

Never hesitate to open your relationship to a qualified person who is more enlightened or clearer than you are at the time. Don't be embarrassed; your willingness can save you years of hassle! I know couples who won't tell anyone they're having problems because they want to "look good." These couples cheat themselves. I've met other couples who never "air dirty laundry." They inherited the conviction from their parents that it's improper to expose anything. Quite frankly, there are times when we cannot solve our problems by ourselves. We need support, and we need someone who is not emotionally involved in the dilemma. An enlightened friend can be a relationship saver. Not only may they offer an unexpected solution, they may guide us to the right rebirther or the right books.

Everyone has problems—don't get upset by yours, just seek out solutions. The dynamic you use for problem solving and achieving solutions should be enjoyable and invigorating, "a win" for you *and* your partner. You should get *high* doing it. If you're exhausted by the process, or feel competitive or resentful about it, you're off track.

When you notice that your old methods aren't working, it's time to figure out a new method that makes life smoother. A good general rule when resolving conflict is *to deal with only one issue at a time*. Resolve the problem under discussion before bringing up others.

When two people can't resolve a major dispute themselves, they may agree to seek the assistance of a mediator. Once, a mediation expert from New Zealand reminded me of a simple but very effective conflict resolution technique that works well in this context. Naturally, it is best to seek someone fairly well-trained in mediating personal conflicts.

The mediator begins by asking one person to give their version of the problem. The other partner listens with complete attention and without interruption, making every effort to see the point of view of the first speaker. As you can imagine, it's harder for a couple to do this alone, since one person may be tempted to interrupt, fight back, or defend. The mediator's presence prevents retorts and interruptions. After the first speaker completes their account, the listener tells their version. This simple step clears the air and takes the pressure off because each party finally feels *heard*. The mediator can then help the couple strive for the highest spiritual thoughts on the subject and complete the process.

Here are some helpful meditations on this subject from *A Course in Miracles*.

- Truth cannot deal with errors that you want to keep.

- It is not up to you to change your brother, but merely to accept him as he is. Any attempt to correct a brother means that you believe correction by you is possible, and this can only be the arrogance of the ego.
- When a situation has been dedicated wholly to truth, peace is inevitable.

TAKING CARE OF YOUR RELATIONSHIP

What do you do when your body starts acting up or breaking down, or gets a sore, a pain, a fracture, an infection? As you know, the wisest course of action is to take care of it *right away*. What happens if you don't? Chances are your body won't heal. What if you still don't tend to it? It may very likely get worse and worse until you have a full-blown disease. If, on the other hand, you're careful to heal each problem as it comes up, you can stay healthy. Your body can work. And if you live a healthy lifestyle and eat well, preventing pains, illnesses, and tensions is even easier. You are enjoying the *vitality* of life. You master your own body and feel great.

Now let's consider *your relationship* in the same way. If you get perturbed with your mate or upset with the relationship, but don't deal with the problem right away, your anger becomes suppressed. If even more resentment piles up on top of the first disagreement, tension builds up. The relationship quickly becomes unhealthy. By neglecting to take care of the "little things," you accumulate poisons in your relationship as you would in your body—and eventually it gets diseased. Left untreated, your relationship grows sicker. By the time you try to get emergency help, it may be too late—the disease has become chronic. Through bitterness, hatred, and attack, it spreads. Soon hostilities run rampant, and the damage appears irreversible. It seems impossible to fix. Separation seems the only way out, as the relationship is dead.

After listening to this all-too-frequent scenario, isn't it quite clear that you need to take time to clear even the *smallest* problem in your relationship? What is the alternative? And does processing it *have* to be hard work? Not if you know clearing techniques that are fun. It can become part of a practical new way of living in which you're clearing your relationship, and your body too, moment by moment.

In healing your body, I would *not* automatically advise you to seek out standard drug-and-hospital-oriented Western medical treatment, which can be so dispiriting. Nor would I advise you to turn exclusively to traditional marriage counseling or expensive psychotherapy when caring for your relationship. As new concepts for holistic health are emerging in modern medicine, they're also emerging in relationship therapy. The emphasis in Western medicine is finally moving in the right direction. As Deepak Chopra points out in his book *Quantum Healing*, medical institutions are at last stressing the healing potential *within* the patient. In other words, the patient himself becomes the physician. In the same way, partners in a couple can learn how to heal their relationship within the relationship itself.

For most of us, our formal education offered no guidance in healing ourselves or our relationships; we cannot look to our schooling for help in these important areas. Instead, we must learn from Infinite Intelligence, others who are more experienced, New Age research—from anywhere possible. The most important principle is to be constantly aware of our need for knowledge and constantly open to learning and correcting ourselves.

The first step in recovering this knowledge involves getting out of denial. How many people deny the truth that their bodies are breaking down or that their relationships are troubled? Denial leads to suppression. Suppression leads to illness and death, misery and divorce. I've met people who walk around in pain every day of their lives, and because they believe that pain is "normal," they do nothing about it. I know couples who quarrel all the time but believe that fighting is "normal," so they don't change. Soon enough, one partner will have an affair and the other is "shocked"—though all the signs were there if they'd paid attention. The same holds true for physical illness. What I'm saying is that when we're dealing with our relationships and our bodies, we *must* look at the writing on the wall. We must identify what is off balance right now and handle it before it's too late.

This advice may sound like nothing more than simple common sense. But it's often wise to rely on your common sense and act on it. How committed are you to living fully, 100 percent of the time? Are you actually more committed to mediocrity, suffering, suppression, pain, lack of joy, and failure? My hunch is that you would prefer joy, excellence, and pleasure. Once you experience how it feels to live a cleaned-up life, you won't tolerate the old way of living much longer.

Another healthy way to help keep your relationship in great shape is to say what you want instead of complaining about what you don't have (a tactic that leads to chronically unhealthy communication). By staying in the positive, you and your mate can then work together to achieve mutual desires. It is far more effective to say, "I would really like to go out together alone at least once a week," than to say "You never spend enough time with me."

Remember, your relationship lives by the same rules your body does: If you mistreat your body rather than give it what it wants and needs, it will eventually break down. And so will your relationship. If you treat it with the care it deserves, you will surely reap the benefits.

Keeping Your Relationship
Clear with Everyone

Ideally, your relationship with another person should be left clear and complete at the end of each encounter. But what about when you're uncomfortable about something that was said—but at the time of the encounter you either didn't realize the exchange upset you, or you "stuffed" your feelings instead of expressing them? If you weren't able to handle it at the time, you should immediately call the person and clear. If they left town, even if they went abroad, you can still call them. Or you may choose to write to them. The important thing is to *stay with* the feeling until both of you feel good and the difficulty is resolved.

Developing the habit of getting things clear on the spot will prove extremely beneficial to your health, self-esteem, and peace of mind. Though you may feel awkward at first, after a while clearing becomes more and more natural. When someone makes a remark that causes discomfort, many of us are accustomed to letting it go and then fuming later. We've been taught that this is the "polite" thing to do. A better way to handle it is to say something like, "What you just said really upsets me. I am willing to look at what my case is about it, but I thought I better tell you right now. Can we talk about it more until this clears?" Or if you can, ask a question such as "Why are you doing this?" and make a clear reference to the upsetting comment or action. Often, when you give other people an opportunity to explain their mindset, their position will make more sense.

When clear, be honest. And *don't* agree with people just to make temporary peace. If you go along with something that bothers you, the conflict will show up later in a skewed form. You will resent having "given in," and this will harm the relationship.

Because any unresolved issues with your parents will come up in your current relationships, clearing with them must be done. To be honest, this is true of all old relationships; we must clean house thoroughly. As impossible as it sounds, we *can* clear all our relationships—the really old ones, the recent past ones, and the current ones. I'm saying that *all* the relationships in your life can work. It's not only possible, it is a must.

You may need to write someone you know a very unenlightened letter steeped in blame, just to release your "charge"—and then burn it afterward. Later, you can compose a more careful version. The final letters should be one where you use "I sentences" such as "I felt this way," rather than "blame sentences" such as "You did that to me." The purpose of the letter should be to restore harmony, not to get even. A good screening method is to have an enlightened friend check to see if the letter contains expressions of covert hostility. The final copy should be a letter you *yourself* would not mind receiving.

CHAPTER 7

ADVANCED RELATIONSHIP DYNAMICS

Your home and the various spaces and objects that comprise it offer a clear, tangible way to measure your level of self-esteem and vitality. Have you ever considered the idea that grime, dirt, filth, and things falling apart represent your *death urge*? Notice the difference in your mood and the vitality of your relationship when your space is pretty and neat. Careful maintenance of your property and belongings creates a cycle of positive energy.

As we develop higher spiritual qualities, we change our vibration. We can make our vibrations magnetic and will attract the best of everything into our lives, including abundance and prosperity. If you don't believe money and spirituality can operate simultaneously, you had best review your belief systems about God. *The Abundance Book* explains that God doesn't provide us with money—he gives us Himself. He gives us *divine substance*, and that substance becomes money, homes, cars, and vacations.

Conflicts over money rank as one of the most frequent causes of divorce, yet they differ little from other ego conflicts. Often it's the attitudes each of us brings to such matters that first need to be cleared. This usually requires positive feedback. If our goal is total illumination, we will welcome the opportunity to see our shadows as soon as they appear. It's best to start a feedback loop from the outset of the relationship. You can give each other permission to point out behavior that doesn't work for either of you.

And the first topic on every couple's list is sex. *A Course in Miracles* would say that with sex, what matters is whether you're in the ego's thought system with it or the Holy Spirit's. If the latter, you would agree with Osho, "The primal energy of sex has the reflection of God in it. Sex is divine." I treat sexual love as a sacrament; its ultimate goal is union with God. As such, I recommend a temple atmosphere for lovemaking with soft music, chanting, and fresh flowers. Would you meet the God in your partner any other way?

And will you find God in your marriage? I once agreed with Bhagwan Rajneesh that this was an outdated institution that destroyed all possibilities for happiness. I have since delved into the subject more deeply and now feel that it's not marriage that erodes relationships but how we respond to each other inside the marriage. It becomes a sacred bond only if it's *made* sacred. Yogananda said, "The desire for marriage is universal because of the cosmic power of love to draw everything back to oneness." Amen.

Children are the natural expression of a love relationship. If you're highly evolved, you can attract a highly spiritual soul. Before conception, send out an invitation to the kind of child you want. During pregnancy, create a spiritual prenatal environment for the soul through spiritual practices and proper care. Know that the imprints for behavior patterns are formed during the prenatal period. And remember that children are developed souls with their own past-life karma, our guests and our gurus.

Your Space and Environment

How does your environment support your relationship? People often laugh at how adamant I am about neatness in regards to their space. But I know from experience that neatness affects your mind and your relationship. When I visit a home, I can instantly determine a family's "aliveness quotient" and also how much they respect each other by the way the home looks. This is not a matter of finances or expensive items; the way you care for your living space reflects how you feel about yourself and those you live with.

Your home and the various spaces that comprise it offer a clear, tangible way to measure your level of self-esteem and vitality.

Let's take the kitchen:

- Is the stove really dirty and the cooking pots all banged up with handles missing?
- Is the food in the refrigerator moldy?
- Are the cupboards a mess?
- Are the sponges in the sink all dirty with dirty dishes stacked up?
- Is there birdseed all over the floor?
- Is the garbage overflowing?

In the living room:

- Are the plants dead?
- Have the cats scratched up all the furniture?
- Are the light bulbs burned out?
- Is the TV dominating everything?

In the bathroom:

- Are the towels rancid?
- Is the shower curtain moldy and the mirror all splattered?
- Do the shower and bathtub have dirty rings?
- Are old bottles lying around?
- Is the bathroom scale rusty?

In the bedroom:

- Is there junk piled around with boxes and items that aren't particularly sensual?
- Are closets bulging with old clothes that are not flattering, or with clothes too small to be an incentive to lose weight? (That will definitely sabotage your self-esteem!)

Why not throw open your closets and try everything on? Then look in the mirror and ask yourself if you like what you see. If the answer is no, give it away. (How do you expect your partner to be turned on if you aren't?) Always dressing nicely, even at home, enhances your mood and sensuality. It's one way a person can show appreciation for their mate. It shows them that you care enough about their opinion to make them feel good by the way you look and the way the house looks.

What about your car?

- Is it all banged up?
- Is it dirty most of the time?
- Is there dog or cat hair everywhere, especially on the seats?
- Are their cigarette butts, gum wrappers, soda cans all around?
- Are there old newspapers and piles of crap on the floors of the car?
- Are major parts of the car not working well?
- Is it really an old wreck?
- What does this say about the way you feel about your body?

And, finally, what about your yard?

- Do you realize that the whole planet is your backyard?
- Why not have a garage sale and get rid of junk in your place?
- Space and silence gives you vitality.

Naturally, you want to feel relaxed in your home. Notice the difference in your mood and the vitality of your relationship when your space is pretty and neat. Maybe you need to hire a housecleaner once a week. Some people clean up household surfaces, but somehow leave *grime* underneath everything. If that describes how you deal with your living space, have you ever stopped to consider the idea that grime, dirt, filth, and things falling apart represent your *death urge*?

I have never understood why people don't fix things immediately instead of letting them go. When you don't fix something right away, you end up with a disintegrating house and broken-down belongings. In time, your home will become a depressing place and yet you'll feel that fixing everything at once is far too expensive. If you wait longer still, you end up feeling run down, and in the meantime your space will have fallen apart.

On the other hand, careful maintenance of your property and belongings creates a cycle of positive energy. When your mind is clear and your thoughts orderly, you want everything fixed. In the same way, when you fix something, you also feel like maintaining yourself and your relationships properly.

Still, a surprising number of people let their houses go until a seemingly impenetrable mess accumulates. When they finally clean it all up, the job exhausts them and they end up taking another repair break for weeks at a time. As garbage builds up, their home becomes a mess all over again; the cycle continues needlessly. It makes much more sense to clean up each thing on the spot, so your space is always neat. For the heavier work, to prevent dirt and grime, hire a cleaning service. If such an arrangement is definitely beyond your means, try pooling your own efforts. The whole family can work together as a cleaning team.

It could be that as a Virgo, I'm extraordinarily obsessed with this topic of cleanliness and order. But, time and time again, I've seen neatness enhance some relationships and neglect erode others.

A couple has to negotiate and work out their own way of doing household chores—a way that really and truly works for both partners. This can get complicated if one mate grew up in a home that was very neat while the other came from one that was rather disorderly. Habits learned in childhood can be a big point of contention—but solutions can still be found. Chores don't have to cause tension. It is fun and easy to work out agreements, try them out, and renegotiate them until both are satisfied.

I once lived with a man who was much neater than I am. If you know me, this may be hard to believe, since I have always had fastidious habits. He, however, was even more particular. A complete perfectionist. He was forever polishing the glass coffee table and dishware, never allowing even *one* coffee cup to sit in the sink! I constantly felt nervous around him. I could never relax. In my eyes, he was obsessed—and of course I considered my standards "just right." After cohabitating for several months, the tension mounted inside me. Several times I almost felt like fighting with him. Luckily, I refrained, and in the end I decided to approach the problem a bit more intelligently. One Saturday morning when he had time to talk, I sat down with him. I said, "I noticed that we have very different styles of neatness. I'm having trouble doing it the way you do it, but maybe if you explain your mindset, it'll help me." When he responded, he truly surprised me. "Well, Sondra, it is really very simple: Prepare every room for God." I was stunned. Between the two of us, his was absolutely the highest thought. I raised my lower thoughts and went up to his and I asked him to help me reach his level. Our relationship taught me a great deal.

MONEY AND RELATIONSHIPS

Conflicts over money rank as one of the most frequent causes of divorce. This news comes as no surprise to most of us, for we know from experience that money is indeed easy to fight about. In any case, money conflicts differ in essence very little from any other kind. The ego loves conflict. When we give up the addiction to conflict and the desire to relinquish peace, we stop fighting about everything, including money. Even issues concerning finances can be resolved peacefully.

Where do we begin solving money conflicts? Each person must start by handling their own "money case." That includes all our negative conditioning about money—conditioning that has affected everything from a lack of prosperity to our addiction to greed and overspending.

You can take all kinds of seminars on money, read any number of books, and learn a whole range of coping methods, but if you don't process your own emotional blocks about money, even the most refined tools and techniques won't work. Or if they appear to solve your present problem, chances are you will later sabotage your financial plans or squander the gains.

When you get too entangled in the material world without first establishing a proper consciousness, the imbalance can cause chaos and disaster. What kind of imbalances can come about? On one end of the scale there is *greed* and on the other end is what we call a *money rejection complex*. Neither of these extremes will bring you happiness. What you want is a reasonable balance.

Greed is an uncontrollable, insatiable appetite for more than you need. Although the person afflicted by greed has no apparent reason, he thinks he must have more and more and more. He strives for it constantly. Greed usually stems from competitive thinking, the idea that one must be better and possess more than another in order to feel worthwhile. Yet, ironically, while accomplishing or acquiring more, the greedy person senses only a greater emptiness, a void which in turn fuels a yearning for even more things. The cycle goes on and on. As my friend Constance said, You'll never be satisfied while you're ruled by greed.

At the other end of the spectrum, a "money rejection complex" stems from the belief that money is sinful or bad, and you therefore block the receipt of money. You will never be satisfied while such thinking persists. Why? Receiving is not selfish. It is simply a completion of a cycle of energy. Money is *innocent*. Isn't it really just paper and energy? Your own energy determines whether or not money flows freely to you. The higher your energy, the more money you can attract and handle. Because your own energy regulates this flow, only you can deprive yourself, and all you receive is entirely up to you as well. Decide that you will receive what you are worth. Learn to think in an unlimited way in general, not just thinking big, but thinking creatively.

As we develop higher spiritual qualities, we change our vibrations. We can make our vibrations magnetic. The task is to become happy first. If we are unhappy with one aspect of our life, it may affect all others. If you truly desire abundance, each area of your life must work. If you're confused about money and spirituality and don't believe the two can operate simultaneously, you had best review your belief systems about God. God is opulent! God is omnipresent wealth!

John Randolph Price, author of *The Abundance Book*, explains that God doesn't provide us with money or homes—he gives us Himself. He gives us divine substance, and that substance becomes money and homes. This substance, or creative energy, flows through the mind of human beings and externalizes itself as a mirror of our thoughts and convictions. Money, he explains, is an *effect*, a by-product of this process. When we concentrate on the effect, we often forget the cause. As we lose sight of the cause, the effect begins to diminish. When we focus our attention on *getting* money, we actually shut off our supply.

The upshot is: If you truly wish to increase your wealth, you must this very moment cease to believe that money is your support, your security, or your safety—money isn't, God is! When you understand and realize this truth, an uninterrupted supply will give rise to abundance. You must look to God alone as the source. Do you want more money, more prosperity in your life? Then transform your consciousness from one of effects—materialism—to one of cause—spirituality.

In a couple, each partner should know thoroughly the financial habits of their own and their mate's family. Mates should help each other to overcome feeling "stuck" rather than clinging to blame.

Many of us believe that we know all we need to know about our mate's views about money. But focused questioning may reveal that our partner's attitudes diverge greatly from what we imagined. This information is crucial because these very attitudes dictate financial decisions affecting both partners.

Too often, money is a taboo subject. I suggest regular, weekly meetings where partners discuss financial affairs, including current agreements, money goals, bills, future economic prospects, savings, fears, and feelings. So if you're fighting about money, stop *now*. What good will that accomplish? Anger blocks money. Guilt blocks money. Sitting down calmly and approaching financial issues in a sober, concerted way diffuses the tension and clears space for other interests. I certainly wish this had been done in my family when I was a child.

It's tempting to avoid looking at the nitty-gritty aspects of our financial affairs. Do you balance your checkbook regularly? Do you make extraordinary purchases on an ordinary budget? Have you "maxed out" a collection of credit cards? Can you distinguish your own financial patterns from your mate's? Are you using a joint bank account to obscure this? The important point is to get a clearer picture of how you use your financial energy.

The God Presence in you provides for your welfare. If you acknowledge that, you will keep on track with money matters. Focus on the lavish abundance of Divine Substance in the whole world.

GIVING AND RECEIVING FEEDBACK
IN THE NEW PARADIGM

Feedback is a delicate and challenging topic. Enlightened beings whose goal is total illumination usually welcome constructive feedback because they want to see their shadows as soon as they appear. Feedback is always good—whether "positive" or "negative." Giving and receiving feedback enlivens a community where people are on a similar spiritual path.

The art of giving and receiving feedback occurs most successfully when people agree to make it happen. In the new paradigm, this is established at the beginning of the relationship. You can open by saying, "You always have my permission to point out behavior that doesn't work for you, or that you believe could be detrimental to me or others. Do I have the same permission from you?"

I personally like feedback—I welcome it! It is one of the reasons I am where I am today. In our spiritual community, we set up situations for this to happen both formally and informally. A formal setting might be a seminar to increase our social and leadership skills. At any time, a participant may stand up and ask for individual feedback on anything from the group, which may then suggest a change in appearance, speaking mode, attitude, or way of relating. The person receiving feedback isn't allowed to defend or debate it. In a more informal setting, such as a private conversation, we may spontaneously tell a person how we feel, trying not to be too harsh or critical. One might say, "Are you aware that you hang up the phone too abruptly? I feel cut off and cut out." (This was feedback I used to hear from others. I wasn't aware of how I made other people feel, and I appreciated knowing. I then had to process why I had developed this habit.)

In intimate relationships, there is a risk of being less tactful, more critical, and too disapproving. This is because we choose mates who are like the members of our family we're angry with. Unfortunately, we project it onto our mates. How can we give each other feedback that is supportive, tender, and sweet? One agreement you can make is to give feedback on the feedback. "I can hear you when you say it like this, but not when you speak in an angry tone—it scares me and I shut down."

Try asking someone why they're doing something a certain way *before* you criticize their action. Sometimes they have a very good reason which refutes your judgment of them immediately. I wish I could always remember to do this! Let's all try to remember: Be curious, not furious.

GIVING FEEDBACK

1. The giver shall first get "permission" to do so, unless you have a prior agreement. Example: "Do you mind if I share with you my feeling about _____?"

2. The giver shall not speak from anger. His heart shall be open as if he were speaking to a best friend with great respect.

3. The giver shall remember that the issue at hand could also be his projection. For example, if the giver says "It feels like you're way too bossy," maybe the other person *isn't*, in fact, bossy but the giver imagines it because his own parents were bossy, or he is himself.

4. The giver should say, whenever possible, "What *I* feel is . . . and what *I* would like from you is. . . ." Speaking in terms of how *you* feel or what *you* want is much better than an accusation.

RECEIVING FEEDBACK

1. The receiver shall keep her heart open and not become defensive. If the feedback is accurate, then she shall be very grateful for it. If the feedback is a projection, then it shouldn't bother the receiver anyway.

2. The receiver shall pay particular attention if she gets this feedback from more than one person. If so, she had better take action quickly.

3. The receiver shall thank the giver instead of defending herself or debating the topic. The receiver may wish to consider adding, "How do you suggest I alter this behavior?"

4. The receiver may take action by asking others to help with clearing this problem more quickly. Example: "So and so says I hang up the phone too fast and cut people off. I don't want to do that. Please support me by telling me whenever I do that with you."

If couples can see that gentle feedback is a huge benefit, they will advance quite rapidly. If, however, the feedback is too critical, hurtful, or upsetting, it can be destructive to the relationship. People do know and can learn the difference. How do you speak to a friend you adore? How do you speak to someone you totally respect? You have to give and receive feedback in the same way. Everyone knows that this is obvious. If you want someone to treat you with respect, you're going to have to treat others that way. It helps always to imagine that your partner is your guru, your teacher, or a holy person you're fortunate to be living with.

Sex in the New Paradigm

With sex, all that matters, according to *A Course in Miracles,* is whether you're in the ego's thought system or whether you are in the Holy Spirit's. If you're in the Holy Spirit's thought system, then it will be a sacred, holy experience.

As Bhagwan Rajneesh has said: "The primal energy of sex has the reflection of God in it. Sex is Divine. It is the energy that creates new life. Therefore you should accept sex with joy and acknowledge its sacredness. When a man approaches his wife, he should have a sacred feeling, as if he were going to a temple. As a wife goes to her husband, she should be full of the reverence one has nearing God. Orgasm is for the momentary realization of *Samadhi.* The ego vanishes. Orgasm is a state of self effacement. *This* is the reason we are really so attracted to it. It is wrong to fill man with antagonism toward sex."

In tantric teachings, sexual love represents sacrament, its ultimate goal is union with God. There are even books on how you and your mate can use tantric sex to achieve physical immortality together (Zitko, 1985).

Immortals can tell you the difference between the "old sex" and the "new sex." They experienced old sex before they understood the concept of physical immortality and worked out their death urge. They had old sex before they learned to rebirth themselves and knew how to use the breath to prolong orgasm, and before the subconscious was cleared of the fear of letting go. New sex is part of their life as immortals. They feel safe enough to handle a lot more energy in the body without the unconscious fear of death. They feel safe enough to let go. Immortals know how to use sex for rejuvenation.

The space a couple chooses for lovemaking should be like a temple. I recommend an altar in the room. I recommend soft music or chanting. I recommend making the whole space as lovely as possible. There should always be fresh flowers, candles, beautiful objects around, and soothing, sensual fabrics. Televisions, library books, stacks of stuff, and old bedding aren't conducive to holiness. Doing a simple puja, or worship, at the altar beforehand will put you in the right frame of mind, even something as simple as waving incense before pictures of the holy ones. Turn the experience over to God.

Think very carefully about your lover. Some teachers will tell you that there can be karmic *exchange* through sexual activity. Sex is not a simple matter of connect-disconnect. Some say that the linking that results from one single sexual activity may last for approximately fourteen months on higher planes, and that the karmic link lasts that long as well. So, think about the consequences before you sleep with someone tonight who may have slept with someone else last night. Sleeping with multiple partners can have karmic as well as bodily consequences. It is important to think about "safe sex" on both a physical and a spiritual level.

MARRIAGE

Many jokes about marriage are very sad. As in the following anecdote, which is meant to be told as a joke, humor acts as a weak cover for cynicism and hurt feelings.

A lady has finished a meal in a hotel coffee shop and asks for her check. Surprised, the waitress exclaims, "But I put your breakfast on the tab of the man sitting next to you, the guy who just left." "What made you do that?" the lady asks, "I don't even know him. I've never seen that man before in my life?" "I'm sorry," the waitress explains, "You two weren't talking to each other so I thought you were married!"

This joke actually reveals an all-too-common phenomenon. Did you know that a psychologist once interviewed 40,000 married couples on communication patterns, and it turned out they talked to each other on average only *27 minutes a week*? Why does marriage so often leave two people so alienated from one another? I've been investigating this question for many years following my divorce, and I must say that most of my findings did *not* make remarriage very appealing.

When actress Glenn Close got pregnant and moved in with her man, reporters asked if she intended to marry. Close responded, "Why should the *government* be involved in this?" Reading her comments, I found that I shared Close's point of view. Yes, I decided, I might get remarried spiritually, but not legally.

During my rebellious stage that followed, I attracted a book called *A New Vision for Women's Liberation.* This book really stirred me up because it contained the most radical statements on marriage I had ever read. The author, Bhagwan Rajneesh, declared that marriage is out of date and that it destroys all possibilities for happiness. He insisted that marriage makes everyone a zoo animal, that it exacerbates the will to die and leads to prostitution. He believes that marriage is an anachronistic barrier that must disappear and that it has ruined the status of women.

Over time, I studied the subject more and more deeply, reading other books such as Swami Kruyananda's *How to Spiritualize Your Marriage,* which *advocated* marriage for another set of reasons. Gradually, I began to feel that the institution of marriage itself was not so negative. At fault were the false notions about what marriage should *mean* and the way people responded to one another once inside the marriage. In other words, marriage becomes a sacred bond only if it is *made* sacred—otherwise it's simply a social contract. Sound reasons for getting married that I read and thought about included these:

- Marriage can help a person achieve inner balance (especially between reason and feeling).
- Marriage helps break the confines of selfishness and the ego, teaching one to live in a larger reality than one's own.
- Marriage helps one expand one's identity.
- It provides a "proving ground" for one's inner spiritual development. It tests a married mate's spiritual qualities.
- Marriage is a vehicle through which one can achieve union with God (after achieving union with the God in your mate).

Pushing ahead, I began looking into Yogananda's teachings on marriage and came across this piece of wisdom: "The desire for marriage is universal because of the cosmic power of love to draw everything back to oneness." The guru stresses how important it is that marriage be based on divine friendship between equals with unconditional love, unconditional loyalty, and the divine qualities of "Kindness, Respect, Trust, and Faith." He prioritized the essential foundations for marriage in this way:

1. Soul unity (similar spiritual ideals and goals and a willingness to attain them through study and self-discipline).
2. Similarity of interests.
3. Physical attraction (which soon loses its attractive power if soul unity and similarity of interest are not present).

How often people reverse these priorities and suffer because of it!
Clearly, marriage is no panacea. Matrimony itself does not solve problems.

In fact, it probably accentuates existing difficulties all the more strongly. Marriage must be manifested in a spiritual context, for if your marriage becomes spiritually stagnant, divorce is likely to be the only possible resolution.

Finally, after reading all sorts of opinions about marriage, I was eager to come to some conclusions on the subject. For me, doing so was particularly difficult because I both agreed with parts of the extremely radical arguments against marriage *and* the sweet spiritual positions that favor it.

In the end, it became evident to me that it isn't marriage, but rather what you *do* with it, that determines whether you achieve liberation or delusion. Because I preferred liberation, I realized that only one question mattered: Am I abiding by the ego's thought system with marriage, which is delusion, or the Holy Spirit's, which is true reality? In other words, *is this a holy relationship or an unholy relationship?*

Let's look at a range of qualities which characterize the two types of union:

UNHOLY RELATIONSHIP VS. HOLY RELATIONSHIP

The ego's mind	The Holy Spirit's mind
Contracts into limited state of self-enclosure	Expands into greater realities
Guiding thought: What can I gain from the other person?	Guiding thought: What can we give to one another?
Reinforces your case (negativity)	Purifies through spiritual discipline, freeing negativity in both partners
Causes clinging, fear, dependency	Causes trust and the freedom to be; reinforcement of self-expansion
Sees the body as a sex object	Sees the body as a temple of God

EGO RELATIONSHIP GOVERNED BY:	SPIRITUAL RELATIONSHIP GOVERNED BY:
Separation	Aliveness
Conflict	Love
Fear	Harmony
Pain	Peace
Anger	Safety
Worry	Certainty
Misery	Trust
Scarcity	Happiness-Joy
Sickness	Perfect Health
Depression	Abundance
Death	Immortality

CHILDREN

If you're planning to have children, there is a fascinating book called *The Child of Your Dreams* that you should read long before conception. Laura Huxley asserts that when conceiving, a spiritually compatible couple has the ability to attract highly spiritual souls. Before conception you can send out an invitation to the kind of child you want. In meditation, you welcome that child. A soul with a love for peace will be attracted to peaceful parents. I have written a book called *Ideal Birth* and suggest that you read it as well as *The Secret Life of the Unborn Child* by Dr. Thomas Verny. Remember that when the child is within the womb, whatever you're feeling and doing is transmitted through vibration into the child.

During the last decade, remarkable headway has been made in the field of pre- and perinatal psychology. One of the most significant findings shows that imprints for tendencies toward dysfunctional behavior in childhood and adulthood are formed during the prenatal period, from conception to birth, and during the first twelve months. This discovery contradicts the previously accepted theory that these imprints develop when the child is one to three years old. Children with reduced prenatal, birth, and perinatal trauma are generally brighter, more alert, intuitive, assertive, and creative. They exhibit independent learning patterns, are clearer about their own needs, display high self-esteem, and score measurably higher on intelligence tests. These differences have been obvious for some time to those of us working in this field and in rebirthing. I thank Margaret Grant, who once sent me a publication called *The Dialogue on Conscious Education*, which is co-sponsored by the Pre- and Perinatal Psychology Association of N.A. and the Task Force on Conscious Education.

Child-rearing is a trying yet fascinating process. I like to remind parents that *children are our gurus*. Youngsters unflinchingly act out our subconscious thoughts, revealing our mind's inner workings. Their unfiltered reactions can teach us a great deal about ourselves and about relating responsibly. The wisest among us will take careful note of what they are saying.

As a parent, it's sometimes hard to conceive of our child's self as separate from our own. But a parent's task is exactly that. One must remember that children are already developed souls from their own past lives. Because children come as guests to their family, one should never attempt to possess a child. As Roger Woolger tells us in his book, *Other Lives, Other Selves*, a child isn't a blank slate at birth. Nor can we delude ourselves into thinking that they have everything to learn from us, or that children are simply helpless creatures. Education isn't a process akin to computer programming. The true meaning of education is "drawing out" by bringing forth the wisdom our children already possess—not by imposing our own will upon them.

There are some guidelines that are especially useful when your child has a problem.

- Don't speak from a feeling of anger.
- Don't let your personal irritation dictate the treatment.
- Focus on how you can help him or her overcome it rather than how it drives you crazy.

Tara Singh offers exceptional advice for parents in her book, *How to Raise a Child of God.*

The child is born with his own space and with his own resources. It is the responsibility of the parent not to intrude on that innocence by putting their own frustrations and knowings on the child. He is born with space. Let the space be.

The function of a parent is to awaken a child to his own eternity, to his own holiness, to the perfection of what God created . . . not to phony books and waste.

A child needs to play . . . mental faculties must awaken in their own internal way and should never be forced. If he is protected from being imposed upon, he will have the discrimination of his own conviction and will not violate what is true within.

It would be so good if you could take your children to a prayer or meditation room in your house . . . a spacious little room uncluttered, with a few cushions, a bowl of water, a plant, and a picture or two of Divine Beings. This room can be alive with purity of space. Take your child into this room every day and come to peace within yourselves.

Here are more of Tara Singh's lovely teachings:

Teach your child not skills, but love to share.

Teach him to have more space in his life, the richness of stillness.

Teach him to widen the gaps of silence between the thoughts with relaxation.

Teach him that all things in their origin are of the one source.

Teach him to pray for his adversary to regain his own peace and harmony.

Teach him not to be controlled by another.

Teach him to bless all things with his peace.

Teach him non-waste and the love of conservation . . . to be a friend of trees, dawn, and twilight.

Teach him simplicity and gratefulness . . . to love virtue.

Teach him to be a friend unto himself.

The purpose of parenthood is to return the child to God. To raise a child of God is to allow God to participate in their upbringing: Would you like to make this civilization truly great? Would you like your children to be able to actualize that dream? Then teach your children this: that *thought is creative.* Negative thoughts produce negative results and positive thoughts produce positive results. Teach them to apply these truths to every aspect of their lives. Insist that schools teach these ideas. (Why didn't we learn that in school in first grade?)

Imagine a civilization where everyone grew up *knowing* these truths and *practicing* them! Start setting an example now. Raise the quality of your own thoughts. Clear out your negative subconscious thoughts. Help your children get to higher and higher thoughts. Let your love guide you.

CHAPTER 8

RELATIONSHIPS IN TRANSITION

If it looks like your relationship is falling apart and you both want to stay together, you need to realize *that it is working* and that you're just locked into a heavy pattern. The love between you is pushing out some negative mass. Consult with someone you trust, or process the relationship using various techniques. You'll never lose anyone who is with you for your highest good.

Some people don't ever want their intimate relationships to change; they wish to stay as they were when they first met. Such couples never experience what they *could become* together. Know that what your mate, or anybody else, wants you to change, are the ego traits that hurt you or others. An enlightened couple desires and welcomes change. Remember that spiritual advancement begins with a radical change of outlook.

A new perspective on relationships may include what is being called "serial monogamy." You commit exclusively to a partner for a significant period of time, but move on if or when the relationship stops growing.

But if the relationship does end, even when you *want* this outcome, it can be painful. I don't like to use the term "breaking up," because relationships never really end, they just change form. Remaining friends can lessen the trauma, especially if you both realize there's something better awaiting you. And know that this is the result you wanted, if unconsciously, for your own growth and development.

I once experienced a very disconcerting breakup with someone I truly loved and respected, who decided one day, without any real reason, to break it off with me. This was just prior to my first trip to India. I consoled myself with the thought that "I have to go to the Master, naked, without attachments." While walking the streets of New Delhi, I heard a voice say, "What if leaving could be a joy?"

"That's ridiculous!" I cried out. I couldn't imagine such a thing.

"Just wait until you see what I have for you next!"

The voice was that of Babaji reminding me that *faith is everything*. Later, I was given *so much* of everything beyond my former life.

"First-Aid" for Your Relationship

First, know that the relationship is working if you both want to stay together. What is happening between the two of you is happening to heal you of something. The love between you is pushing out some negative mental mass. Another way of saying this is that your patterns are "dovetailing." Instead of yelling and screaming at one another, take one of these alternatives:

1. Consult with someone you trust.
2. Call your local Rebirther and make an appointment.
3. Write down all your negative thoughts and turn them into affirmations.
4. Become aware of all your blame thoughts about the other. Remember that blame is always misguided. All disapproval is projection; your partner is your mirror. What does this say about you? How did you create this? How did you attract this?
5. Remember that love is bringing up what's unlike itself. Don't leave until you understand the pattern at least, or you will just recreate it with the next person.

6. Handle your anger in individually appropriate ways.

7. Remember that you're never upset for the reason that you think. Get in touch with the earlier situation you're reliving.

8. Lie down and hold each other. When you can't communicate, *stop* and hold each other and breathe together gently.

9. When you've calmed down, share all feelings, one at a time. One person talks, the other listens without interrupting.

10. Take a relationship training course. See my web site: SondraRay.com.

If your mate is with another woman or another man and you're blaming them both, *stop*. Sit down alone and tell yourself the truth. Try writing the following phrases at the top of a piece of paper and see how many items you can list for each one.

1. The reasons I attracted this situation are . . .

2. My payoff for creating this mess is . . .

3. What I get to prove to myself is . . .

4. What that other person represents is . . .

5. The reasons I secretly want my mate to do this are . . .

6. The thoughts I have been thinking that created this are . . .

7. The thoughts that will clear up my jealousy are. . . . Since your partner is your mirror, it's possible that you secretly want to go out with someone else. Maybe you resent that others have the pleasure you won't allow yourself. Or you may be pulling in a person who represents a sibling who stole the attention of one of your parents (i.e., you're setting up your partner as your parent).

If the relationship falls apart despite everything you have tried, and your partner leaves you, remember this: You never lose anything or anyone who was with you for your highest good under any circumstances. If you've lost someone, then that person was no longer a part of your highest good.

The best news is this: Nothing is ever taken from you without it being replaced by something greater. In this situation, God is trying to give you something better, so *let go*. You must create a vacuum to receive the new.

ALL LOSSES ARE GAINS NOT RECOGNIZED.

THE FEAR OF CHANGE

We must now re-examine the idea of change and what it really means. We aren't talking about changing the Real Self. It needs no change. What needs to change is the *idea* of who you are—the ego's idea of limitation. If you consider it in those terms, why wouldn't you want to change? What your mate, or anyone else, wants you to change, are the parts that are illusions—the traits that hurt you or others. People who are threatened when someone insists that they change don't understand this point.

Some people don't ever want their intimate relationship to change. Some couples think they should stay as they were when they first met. But they will never experience what they *could become* together!

Many articles on relationships imply that a man can change only if a crisis in his life triggers it. And furthermore, what influences a man to change better not be his lover! Warning after warning is given that if a man is under pressure to change at home, he'll feel more secure with a mistress who likes him as he is. Some advise that if you want to keep a man, never ever criticize him. I've been reading this for decades. There is actually some truth to it, *if* the man is operating in the old paradigm.

I certainly don't recommend criticism. What I *do* suggest is opening up to a New Paradigm where conscious willingness to advance is one of the main components. This means you have to change—especially your limitations and your ego-based negative thoughts. An enlightened couple desires and welcomes change. They welcome feedback. They know, with certainty, that we've all been asleep spiritually, that we need to wake up. The word for couples to focus on would be ENCOURAGEMENT. Each encourages the other to advance.

Spiritual advancement begins when there is a radical change in the outlook of a worldly person. The pursuit of the body's desires is no longer a motivating factor. To the spiritually advanced person, the values of the soul predominate. Then the body is used as an instrument to help achieve this advancement.

When you attempt to jump to a new level of consciousness, the ego puts up a battle. Fear has to be confronted. You need effective tools to deal with it. In rebirthing, we inhale love and exhale fear. We say, "Fear Forward!" Fears are due to thoughts—thoughts that can be *changed*. If you're resistant to changing old habits and addictions, then you need to clear, or "process," the fear of letting go of these crutches. Rebirthers are trained to help you with this struggle.

Sometimes, people are afraid of change because their first big change was going from the comforting liquid darkness of the womb to the harshly lit atmosphere of the delivery room. This memory remains somewhere within them. Rebirthing can work out such birth trauma.

TWO APPROACHES

One approach is the "staying together no matter what" approach. This involves the "till death do us part" attitude of the old paradigm.

Then there is the second approach, called "serial monogamy," in which a person commits exclusively to a partner for a significant period of time, but moves on if and when the relationship stops growing. They go on to commit exclusively to another partner for another unspecified period of time, and so on. People who can handle this approach don't feel guilt about having short relationships. They feel it is illogical to think that one partner is going to suit them for many decades. They may even say at the beginning of a relationship that they're not promising that they will feel the same way in ten years time.

This may be hard for many of us to accept. However, those of us seeking new paradigms will say that it's a lot more honest than having multiple affairs. Serial monogamy isn't suited for everyone, however. Psychotherapist Diana Laschelles states that this relationship pattern only suits confident people who are socially very comfortable and can separate easily, recover fast, and move on. Some admit that there is a danger of becoming jaded. Others complain that this system cannot work when children are involved. Still others think it can; they say it isn't good to teach children to stick together in "martyred misery." (Laschelles, January 1994)

It remains to be seen whether people will find ongoing satisfaction with this lifestyle, but it needs to be discussed, as it is becoming more and more common. What I find most interesting about discussions on this subject is that people usually say that if their relationship stayed truly alive, they would not mind staying in it forever. They don't seem to want serial monogamy just for its own sake or just for variety. What people seem to be searching for is something that doesn't die.

You can use the serial monogamy approach or you can try to stay in the same relationship forever. The choice is yours. Either way, one has to learn how to keep these relationships alive. Keeping your relationship alive requires enlightenment.

Achieving enlightenment also has two approaches. The traditional way is to simply let life itself process you. By going through the "school of hard knocks," and by experiencing life after life of numerous incarnations, the soul is finally forced to achieve enlightenment. It wakes up completely and becomes whole. The problem is that this approach is very slow, especially if one isn't conscious that enlightenment is the goal.

The second approach makes a conscious choice to commit to self-analysis and spiritual purification on a regular, daily basis—dissolve and be reborn again each day. To me, this is easier, quicker, more wonderful and *the point of this book.*

THE END OF A RELATIONSHIP

No one wants to contemplate a relationship ending—and with good reason. If you dwell on it, worry about it, or fear it, you give it energy and a separation may well occur. What you believe to be true, you create. What you fear, you attract. If you believe all relationships will end, then that is what you create.

Ending a relationship, even when you *want* this outcome, causes considerable pain. If you didn't want it to end and it did anyway, the pain may seem insurmountable. How do you get through that difficult period without intolerable pain?

As I have said many times, if someone leaves, they're no longer the best partner for you; the universe is trying to give you something better! Nothing is taken from you without it being replaced with something better. If you remember these truths, the disappointments won't hit as hard. If you release the thought "There is nobody else out there," it will be easier. You cannot receive the great good that is coming until you let go of your attachment.

I don't like to use the term "breaking up." It seems too harsh, and, more importantly, I don't believe that relationships ever really *end*, they just change form. To better handle the potential trauma of separation, make it less of a crisis. If you and your longtime mate decide to separate, you can remain friends. It is the form of your relationship that changes. At first this may be hard. You feel too sensitive and contact is too painful. But talk about it as a possibility for later on. If you keep your heart shut down toward someone, it hurts you. Give yourself some time to recover, but remember your mate is your teacher, your healer, and, in the end, the only appropriate response toward them is gratitude. To help you with this attitude, I recommend you read *A Course in Miracles*.

Remember that the failure of your relationship may actually be to your benefit. Failures can be gains not recognized: no matter what the result of your relationship, you wanted that result! You may not be consciously aware of it, but you're always getting what you want. Even if you failed, you wanted to fail: either to reconfirm a part of your ego, to have an excuse to get angry, or to have something to blame. Because you wanted to fail, you succeeded at failing; therefore, you were really a success. Even if you don't comprehend this logic at the time, you will later, so you might as well accept it sooner! It can only ease your mind.

LETTING GO WITHOUT BITTERNESS

I would like to relate a very special story about how my Master, Babaji, helped me to recover from hurt relationships—and this was before I even met him! (I now realize that I had been with him in another life that I didn't remember.) In any case, this story takes place in *this* lifetime.

At the time I had first planned to go to India, I was a newly certified rebirther having a great relationship with another rebirther. My partner had become a trainer with me, and we traveled together working as a team. We had been involved with each other for two years, when one day he came home and simply said to me, "I have to leave." I was shocked. I thought we were getting along very well. I asked him, "Why? Are you upset with me?" And he answered, "No." "Are you upset with our relationship?" Again, he said, "No." Then he said, "I just have to leave." And so he did. No explanation was given and I never saw him again. That same week other things began to fall apart as well. A friend wrecked my sports car and left it lying in a ditch. And the beautiful home where I had been living was suddenly sold, and I was informed that I must vacate immediately. I had lost everything I was attached to.

Though I was trying to be enlightened and to "handle it," in truth I was very shaken. For days I felt as if my feet never really touched the ground. The shock entirely erased my travel plans from my mind. Then, one morning after yet another night of fitful sleep, I woke up and remembered that I was going to India. "Oh, I get it," I thought. "I have to go to the Master, naked, without attachments." All the losses I'd just experienced finally made sense. Calmer now, I pulled myself together and left for Asia.

Weeks later, walking along in New Delhi, I found myself painfully yearning for my former partner. Indulging in my loneliness, I only made myself miserable. Then, suddenly, I heard a voice—the voice was part of a "presence" I felt to the right of me. I asked, "What if leaving could be a joy?" "That is ridiculous!" I cried. I couldn't imagine such a thing. But as much as I resisted this presence, it seemed only to grow. Finally, it spoke again, "Just wait until you see what I have for you next!" I was so startled that I fell to the ground, humbled; I wept and finally spoke in a whisper, "Pardon me for my little faith." Rising, I left for the Himalayas, where I would come to understand everything.

It was only later that I learned the voice I had heard in the streets of New Delhi was that of Babaji. He was reminding me that when something or someone leaves us, it is no longer best for us, and that nothing is taken from us without it being replaced by something better. Babaji taught us that *faith is everything*. Later, I was given *so much* of everything beyond my former life.

If a relationship ends and you feel dispirited because you didn't want that outcome, it may be valuable to do a truth process by completing a sentence such as, "The reason I wanted to have this relationship end was _____." This exercise is *especially* helpful if you wanted the bond to continue.

The truth is that "results are your guru." Even though you may not yet realize it, you *did* in fact want it to end. *A Course in Miracles* reminds us to be aware of the temptation to perceive ourselves as unjustly treated. No one can hurt you but yourself!

A period of grieving is, of course, natural. But you can shorten it by nurturing your self-esteem. Remember that you can go out and create new relationships whenever you like. If you're a woman, you don't have to wait around for men to ask you out. You can also cut down the grieving time through spiritual purification. (See *Pure Joy*)

I believe it is important to refrain from judging yourself adversely if you have a series of brief relationships instead of fewer, longer ones. Shorter relationships aren't automatically "bad." Sometimes you need people to come into your life for shorter periods. Each will be your guru for a time, followed by the next, who will also serve as your teacher. The important question is this: Have you become more loving with each new experience?

Marianne Williamson talks about various alternatives on her excellent tapes about relationships and *A Course in Miracles*. Listen to them instead of moping around. Get going on a new life. There are new people to meet, new experiences to relish; joy is just around the corner. The whole idea is to create a sense of *inner joy* that doesn't depend on exterior circumstances going well.

CHAPTER 9

SPIRITUAL DYNAMICS IN RELATIONSHIPS

It's important to be aware of reincarnation and karma to have a deeper understanding of what is happening in your life and in your relationships to others. Instant attractions and repulsions are usually based on karmic ties, as are love/hate obsessions of any kind.

We have to choose not to allow unconscious behavior to continue—and it takes the willingness of *both parties* to clear up an abusive relationship. *A Course in Miracles* says, "You're never upset for the reason you think." Remember that every upset is a "set up" to allow each person to examine his or her part in creating it. And no matter what happens, clearing the atmosphere afterward is a major test of your spiritual qualities.

It's not always easy to respect someone when you don't approve of their behavior. To keep your partner's respect, be willing to see your shadows and work on them. To maintain respect for them, remember: Shadows aren't real. They're like the cobwebs covering up the Real Self. In a committed relationship, you both have every problem, even if it seems to show up *over there*.

The *kahunas* of Hawaii teach that criticism of the self or others causes stress and inhibits awareness, memory, and energy flow. To break the habit of judging people, try blessing the situation instead. Bless the person moving through offensive behavior, and see them as healed of it and honor and respect their God Self. *Blessing* what you want daily and focusing on *praise* as a habit will create a safe place in your relationship. Attitudes of love, praise, and gratitude fill one with the power of the Spirit.

To worship means to "revere the worth of" something or someone. When we worship a person, we see no wrong in him or her whatsoever. We open ourselves to them completely. To receive our brother's or partner's wisdom, we must pay careful attention to how we worship. Devotions cleanse our being and bring us nearer to the Holy Spirit. They enhance your relationship and your whole life.

How often have you, as part of a couple, had the experience of true bliss together, but just couldn't maintain it? Something happened and you came crashing down. You shouldn't give up your intention of experiencing bliss. What you intend, you become. Crashing simply means that more of your ego has been processed. So long as you stay on the path to total enlightenment, your periods of bliss will be longer. I return to the Himalayas every year to experience those saints constantly in bliss to know it's possible.

Handling Karmic Debts and Dues

Self-analysis and processing are frequently underestimated because people are often unaware of the laws of reincarnation and karma. An understanding of these laws contributes immeasurably to the process of emotional clearing. These laws are an integral part of the Rebirthing community's paradigms.

The spiritual master Yogananda says, "Reincarnation is the progress of a soul through many lives on the earth plane, as through so many grades in a school, before it 'graduates' to the immortal perfection of oneness with God." He also says that in order to comprehend the justification of man's apparent inequalities, we must first understand the law of reincarnation. Knowledge of this law was lost in the West during the Dark Ages. Yogananda says Jesus spoke of this law when he said, "Elias is come already; and they knew him not." (Elias reincarnated as John the Baptist.) Yogananda points out that, without reincarnation, there would be no divine justice operating for those souls who have not yet had a chance to express themselves, such as a baby born dead (Yogananda, 1982).

If there were no law of cause and effect in the physical world, all would be chaos. Meher Baba says:

All that has happened in past lives does have its own unconscious, but effective, share in determining one's actions and responses in this life. Fate is really man's own creation pursuing him from past lives. Karmic determination is the condition of true responsibility. It means that an individual will reap what he sows. According to Karmic Law he can neither avoid the debts or the dues. It is through his own binding karma that he invites upon himself pleasure or pain. He keeps reincarnating to pay off his debts and recover his dues. But even then he may be unable to clear his account for two reasons: (1) All the persons with whom he or she has karmic links may not be incarnate when he has taken a body. (2) Due to particular limitations of his capacities or circumstances, he or she may not be able to meet all the complex circumstances. He may even go on adding to his debts or dues (i.e., creating NEW karma!). The result could be that there is difficulty getting out of his complex karmic entanglements. These entanglements would be endless if there were no provisions for release. The help of a Perfect Master is enormous for this. The Perfect Master can bring emancipation. Another way out is spiritual purification and service to humanity." (*Discourses*, pp. 334–337)

It is very important to be aware of the concepts of reincarnation and karma so that you may have a deeper understanding of what is happening in your life, yourself, and in your relationships with others. If you meet someone new and you feel instantly repulsed by him or her, perhaps you share some bad karma. If you meet someone and you experience instant camaraderie, perhaps you have shared wonderful past lives with this person. The same dynamic holds true for entire countries. What parts of the world have you always wanted to visit? Are there other places you would *never* travel to? Clear it. Go!

TRANSMUTING UPSETS

There are times when one or both partners forget about the techniques discussed and just "lose it" or "blow it" with each other. When either of you has what I call an "ego attack" that results in a fight, you are *both* left with the task of cleaning it up. How you handle this task is all-important to the future well-being of your relationship. You can either create more separation or you can become even closer. The outcome is your responsibility. Train yourself to remember that, "You are never upset for the reason you think," as *A Course in Miracles* would say. If one of you can be quiet and just let the other vent all of his or her feelings, then maybe you can ask, "What is *really* bothering you?" If just one of you can drop the rope, the tug-of-war will be over. LET IT BE YOU.

No matter what happens, cleaning up afterward is a major test of your spiritual qualities. Safety is the complete relinquishment of attack; if you don't retract, the person who feels attacked may become so afraid that he or she will just withdraw in the future. Apologies are in order ASAP!

Leonard Orr, the founder of Rebirthing, once said, "The only way to have a perfect relationship is to have two people willing to experience their own perfection." This must be the goal for each partner: A willingness to keep perfecting oneself by self-improvement. Each must remember that this is the purpose of life—and it is a spiritual purpose. So, a couple must make self-improvement a top priority. Once this is established and followed, it becomes much easier to transmute upsets.

Every upset is a "set up." Each person in the upset has to examine his or her part in creating it, *without exception*. When *both* partners take responsibility, healing occurs. This is harder to do when one person "looks" innocent on the surface, and the other "looks" guilty. In a violent situation, like spousal abuse, you may find it very hard to understand how this applies. In this case, you may need to muster up enough self-love to physically leave the abusive situation. The problem is, of course, that if you don't discover (through self-realization) how you might've attracted, or been attracted to, this kind of situation, it could be recreated in the next relationship.

One of my teachers in India asked me to help a couple in an abusive marriage. I cringed at this assignment knowing it was going to be very hard. I agreed because I needed to learn more about this dynamic, and I liked the two people involved. I was also the one who had "discovered" the abuse. I began by rebirthing each of them separately. The man had a basic negative thought, "I AM BAD" (personal lie), from his birth script, which led to bad behavior, like hitting his wife. The negative reinforcement allowed him to continue to feel bad about himself. The basic negative birth thought of his wife was, "I AM WRONG," a built-in belief that demanded punishment. She believed that she deserved the abuse that followed and would feel that she was wrong to protest it. Years later, after the abuse pattern was cleared, the wife told me that her addiction to smoking was both a punishment and a cover-up for her feelings. She had since given up smoking, which was hard, but not as hard as giving up the addiction to getting herself beaten up. However, the hardest addiction to overcome was the thought "I AM WRONG."

We have to choose not to allow unconscious behavior to continue—and it takes the willingness of *both* parties to clear up an abusive pattern in a relationship. Forgiveness is the key to happiness but, in the new paradigm, we would honor *A Course in Miracles* definition of forgiveness. You don't forgive the old way by implying, "You did this horrible thing, but I am going to be righteous and forgive you anyway." In other words, you don't pardon sins by making them real. You see that there was no sin. You recognize that what the other person did wasn't real.

A Course in Miracles states, "Every loving thought is true and all else is an appeal for help." This means that even the most offensive action is a twisted way of asking for help. Try to remember this; God asks us to remember this.

Who has offended you recently? Why not call this person and ask him or her how you can be supportive? Try it! If you love the offending person unconditionally anyway, the conflict is over for you. If correction is in order, offer it from love, not judgment.

We used to ask Babaji at the ashram in India why he had allowed thieves to stay there. He said, "Who else is going to love them?"

MAINTAINING RESPECT

It is easy to respect someone who impresses you or is doing what you think they should do. But what about when you don't approve of the other person's behavior—do you lose complete respect for that person? When respect disappears from a committed relationship, the partners often give up and look elsewhere.

To keep your partner's respect, be willing to see your shadows and be willing to work on them. To maintain respect for them when their shadows are displayed, remember this: Shadows aren't real. They're like cobwebs covering up the Real Self. The Real Self is God. The Real Self is Love. If you choose to disrespect someone because of their shadows, then you're making their shadows real—you're, in fact, reinforcing them.

Once when a friend came to visit me, I had a spontaneous reaction to what seemed to me his lack of feeling. I started crying. He felt he should leave because I was so distraught. I couldn't stop the upset but, as it started to escalate, my companion lay down on the floor near my altar, and I was able to reach over, touch him, and say: "I don't care about this. I just want you to know how much I respect you." This cut right through it. I wanted him to know that I wasn't losing respect for him. He took my hand and told me how much he respected me. It worked. I felt I had to say it out loud. I didn't want him to feel shame, especially since I was still unaware of my part in the upset. In the morning, as we were rebirthing in the hot tub, I told him I could see how I was setting him up like one of my family members. I apologized. (Projections happen fast—you have to always be on guard. It takes self-awareness.)

Maintaining respect for someone when they're having a money problem can be very difficult. You might blurt out something horrible like, "You call yourself a man? Why can't you make a decent living?" At such times it is absolutely crucial to remember that your mate is acting out your father, your mother, or your hidden shadow. You need to find out why this money situation is in your life. If this is a committed relationship, you have to solve the problem together; the first step is to see that you *both* have the problem, even if it is seemingly showing up *over there*.

An example: If a lover refuses to commit and yet I want total commitment, then I have several choices. He could be the part of me that's afraid to commit and won't. I could be the part of *him* that really wants to commit. His refusal to commit may be a mirror to show me that my mind isn't, in fact, undivided on this subject. I need to respect him for being a mirror.

In some cases, you have to leave a relationship in order to maintain your own self-respect, but you must always follow up with self-analysis on your personal agenda.

Blessing Instead of Judging

Although blessing instead of judging is an ancient practice, it might be new for you to bless those whom you want to judge.

The *kahunas* of Hawaii teach that even mentally criticizing others affects your body. They teach that criticism of the self or of others causes stress and inhibits awareness, memory, and energy flow, making you weaker and more susceptible to illness.

The Bible teaches us that someone who is thankful for everything will be made glorious and that attitudes of love, praise, and gratitude fill one with an incomprehensible power of the Spirit. These are called the "ascension attitudes."

We may know these ideas, but applying them at all times can be challenging. When someone displays a behavior that is intolerable, we usually don't feel like praising them. To break the habit of judging that person, try blessing the situation instead. Support the person who is moving through the offensive pattern, bless them, see them as healed of it, and honor and respect their God Self. This is easier to do if the relationship is already placed in the context of conscious blessing.

Blessing what you want *daily* and focusing on *praise* as a habit will create a safe space in your relationship. A sense of peace and relaxation should be the context of any relationship; and this should be re-established daily—telepathically and verbally. If a couple makes a point of focusing on praise as a daily discipline, preferably in a sacred space (such as before an altar), then everything that happens is placed in that context. When that context is repeatedly re-established, each partner becomes more willing to resolve issues and work out his or her own dark shadows with the support and encouragement of the other. If your mate knows, with certainty, that you continually bless him and don't judge his true being or self, he won't be threatened by discussing those actions or habits that need to be corrected for him to become totally enlightened.

However, if someone has come from a home where criticism and verbal abuse were common, he may not only expect criticism, but may try to draw that same behavior out of his mate. The mind seeks familiarity. He may unconsciously want criticism and judgment so that he will "feel at home." Or he may want it to feel the familiar resentment. Praise and gratitude might even seem suspicious to a mind addicted to criticism. This self-induced pattern is an obstacle that must be overcome. Enlightened couples must become aware of this obstacle and deal with it together.

Start by blessing everything and by practicing *praise saturation.*

BLESSING SITUATIONS

Let's say you find yourself in a place you don't like but from which there is no escape. You feel like complaining. Instead, ask yourself "Why have I created this situation? What can I learn from it?" Then ask yourself "How can I lift the resonance here?" The answer is to bless the place and the situation as your teacher and to bless it as valuable even though it may not have met your standard of quality and beauty. You may actually bring about a change. You can also bless everyone and everything that represents what you want. Creating verbal blessings is a way to express gratitude, create powerful affirmations, and take responsibility for shifting negative energy.

PRAISE SATURATION

Many people have no idea how great they are. Perhaps they've had a lot of parental disapproval. They may be starved for acknowledgment. Praise saturation merely means you acknowledge them verbally in every way you can think to do—and you do it sincerely, finding those qualities that are really great and true in that person.

Praise saturation can be done formally or informally. In a formal approach, you would seat the person before a group. Each member or "praiser" in the group tells this person something they like and appreciate about him or her. Continue until a saturation point is reached (as long as you feel it is right). Say whatever truthful thought comes to mind:

"Something I really like about you is your upbeat attitude and positive energy."

"Something else I really like about you is your passion for life."

"Something else wonderful about you is your ability to stay calm and focused in a crisis."

Informally, you can do this anytime and anywhere with anyone. Make sure the person hears these acknowledgments. When a family member accomplishes something good, it is very important to acknowledge and bless them so they can reinforce the manifestation of this good quality. Try it.

DEVOTION: WORSHIPPING TOGETHER AS A COUPLE

When we worship we "revere the worth of" something or someone. Worship is natural, the highest, most nonjudgmental form of love, and to refrain from it is unnatural.

When we worship a person, we see no wrong in him whatsoever. We open ourselves completely to him. If we worship a teacher, we'll learn very quickly, for we'll be open and receptive to all he has to say. To receive our brother's wisdom, we must pay careful attention to the *way* in which we worship; for discriminatory worship leads us down a meaningless path. Instead, we must worship *all of life,* for equality is the only truth. Through worship we gain the most out of life and feel the very best we can. Through worship we contribute to a more advanced civilization.

Once you clarify you own ideas about worship, which may have been muddled by traditional religious perspectives, you can then start over with a fresh perspective on worship and devotion. Create your own forms and your own altar honoring your most sacred feelings.

Devotions cleanse our being and bring us nearer to the Holy Spirit. Here are some suggested devotions you can do with your partner. They will enhance your relationship and your whole life:

- Breathing together
- Reading *A Course in Miracles* aloud to each other (try reading it one week in place of the newspapers, which provoke more internal conflict)
- Chanting together
- Meditating together
- Writing affirmations together
- Fasting together
- Appreciating silence together
- Praying together, out loud or in silence
- Fire purification together
- Visiting holy places together
- Listening to spiritual music together
- Shaving your heads at the same time
- Going to a sweat lodge or float-to-relax tank together
- Attending seminars together
- Spreading enlightenment and networking together
- Committing to a Peace Project together

THE GOAL OF STABILIZATION OF BLISS

How often have you, as part of a couple, had the experience of true bliss together, and wanted to stay there, but just couldn't? Something happened and you came crashing down. It was a devastating feeling. You long to return to bliss. Is this not one of the reasons we might become so addicted to sex? Sex gives us but a momentary experience of what *Samadhi* is like.

We don't have a lot of experience with Bliss Consciousness. If you try to imagine a couple in bliss most of the time, you may find it difficult, if not impossible. We have no reference point from the past to back up this idea as a real possibility. We have very few experiences of staying in bliss with another person, or even alone. Because of these past experiences, we may end up with the subconscious thought, "If I'm in bliss now, something terrible will happen later." (I will fall out of bliss.) We become scared of this feeling and the fear pushes bliss farther away—yet we still long for it! You have to look at why this is: "Love [bliss] brings up anything unlike itself." In other words, the bliss of love will bring up the opposite, which is the ego. Bliss, like love, "triggers" ego material that needs to be processed. (Isn't that why great sex drives people nuts?)

You shouldn't give up your intention of experiencing bliss. What you intend, you become. Every time you achieve a blissful state and crash afterward, it simply means that more of your ego has been processed—it doesn't mean it's impossible to keep your bliss. So long as you stay on the path to total enlightenment, eventually your periods of bliss will be longer and the crashes will become shorter and less painful. Most spiritual masters who are in bliss all the time worked very hard to attain it. It's a process of unraveling the mind, and it's a long process.

In Meher Baba's profound book, *Discourses*, he carefully explains the stages of the Path. There are seven stages of advancement before the soul gets to Permanent Bliss, or total annihilation of the ego (a humbling process!). This chapter has greatly increased my respect for the true spiritual path.

One of the reasons I return to the Himalayas every single year is to experience (and vibrate toward) those saints who are constantly in bliss. I need a reality check. I need to know it is possible. I have no framework or model for bliss elsewhere in my life.

In spiritual life, this is called the *principle of right association* or putting yourself in contact with the highest, most blissful people possible for as long as you can tolerate it. You're forced to adapt upward! (In other words, be careful who you hang out with. Or you might be tempted to match energies with lower vibrations.)

SPIRITUAL RELATIONSHIPS

CHAPTER 10

When we regard one individual as more "special" than anyone else, more valuable than ourselves, even more precious than God, *A Course in Miracles* identifies this as a "special relationship." But, as children of God, all human beings together comprise the *Sonship*. In coveting a special relationship, we limit our love to one small segment of the Sonship. We deny our need for God and believe this special relationship can offer us salvation.

Completion only comes from union with God and from the extension of that union to others. The *Course* tells us "you have no meaning apart from your rightful place in the Sonship, and [the] rightful place of the Sonship is God." Ironically, when a crisis destabilizes our lives—just when we need the support of others—a strange "pull" separates us from friends and family. "Alone we can do nothing," the *Course* states. "Our function is to work together."

"You cannot enter God's presence . . . alone. . . . All your brothers must enter with you." And when we accept our brother *unconditionally*, we open the door to loving all of humanity. Loving our brothers, loving the Holy Spirit, and loving ourselves is *one and the same*. "As you come closer to a brother, you approach me, and as you withdraw from him I become distant to you. Salvation . . . cannot be undertaken successfully by those who disengage themselves from the Sonship."

If we develop our consciousness to the level required, we can be in love with everyone. I'm recommending intimacy—emotional and spiritual intimacy. That is what a spiritual master does. He falls in love with everyone. And loving everyone isn't a threat to either partner in an enlightened relationship, because each understands that the Holy Spirit is in everyone. God is not impartial, so why are we? In a Community of Majesty, intimacy with everyone occurs naturally.

Imagine belonging to a group of fabulous people who are working on enlightened projects together and helping each other to become healed, happy, and whole. Imagine people who actually express their Christ-nature! I envision a paradigm in which you and your mate are part of such a supportive group. It is important to belong to a spiritual family when you're breaking cultural traditions. The Hawaiian's call this family the *ohana*, which means "chosen family who breathes together."

My spiritual master Babaji encourages us to live a life of truth, simplicity, love, and service to mankind. This will change your life for the better. Selfless service means that you're willing to give up personal motives. It is also necessary to have spiritual understanding. Sometimes we need to allow others to find their own way. When my husband and I joined the Peace Corps, we were deeply touched by this experience. This was my "boot camp" that helped me leap into world service.

HOLY VS. UNHOLY RELATIONSHIPS

I always encourage everyone to read the entire *A Course in Miracles* over and over again. This essay will summarize what the *Course*'s teachings say on the subject of relationships. Though, in fact, the entire *Course* concerns relationships, I've concentrated on chapters 15, 16, 17, 20, and 22, which discuss the tyranny of the "special relationship." The *Course* also identifies what it calls the "special hate relationship." It warns us not to be afraid of looking at these darker and more difficult relationships, for our freedom rests on our ability to address them (paraphrase, Text, p. 313).

The *Course* explains that, in a special relationship, we regard one individual as more "special" than anyone else, more valuable than ourselves, and even more precious than God. But this idea is a delusion. As children of God, all human beings together comprise the *Sonship*. In coveting a special relationship with one human being, we limit our love to only one small segment of the Sonship, and are inevitably aware that we have forsaken the totality of that Sonship. This brings guilt into our relationship, and guilt houses fear.

The special love relationship is a compelling distraction we use to obscure our attraction to God the Father. In other words, within the special relationship, we deny our need for God by substituting the need for special people and special things. Hope of salvation depends solely on one individual, and so the attention our partner may devote to activities outside the relationship feels like a threat to our well-being. Because special relationships delude us into believing they can offer salvation, we also accept the erroneous idea that *separation is salvation*. In fact, such exclusive relationships serve as the ego's chief weapon in barring us from a heavenly existence.

An unholy relationship feeds on differences; each partner perceives that his mate possesses qualities or abilities he doesn't. On the surface, such a partnership seems to bear out the old claim that "opposites attract." Upon closer inspection, however, a different picture emerges. In reality, each partner enters into such a union with the idea of *completing themselves and robbing the other*. They each remain in the relationship only until they decide that there is nothing left to steal, and then they move on.

Within these kinds of relationships, whatever reminds a person of past grievances attracts them. I call this "being attracted to your patterns." It's obvious these partners aren't there out of a wish to join with their mate in Spirit. More surprising, however, is the fact that they aren't even attempting to join with the *body* of their mate. Instead, they seek a union with the bodies of those *who are not there* (paraphrase, Text, p. 331)—such as their father or mother or others. Based on these impulses, this unholy bond has little to do with real love. This attempt at union ultimately excludes the very person with whom the partnership was made (paraphrase, Text, p. 321).

The special love relationship also has a flip side. In the special hate relationship, negative impulses are merely more transparent, for the relationship is clearly one of anger and attack. In this arrangement, one person becomes the focus of our anger; we hold on to everything they've done to hurt us. The special hate relationship wreaks vengeance on the past. It holds the past against us (paraphrase, Text, p. 323). And it involves a great amount of pain, anxiety, despair, guilt, and attack (paraphrase, Text, p. 317).

Every special relationship you've made is a substitute for God's will, and glorifies your own instead. Every special relationship harms you by occupying your mind so completely that you cannot hear the call of Truth.

This relationship is based on the assumption that something within us is lacking and therefore we have special needs. To satisfy these needs, we come to believe that another individual is capable of giving us what is missing in ourselves. A conviction of our own littleness lies at the heart of every special relationship, for when two mates endeavor to become one entity, they've forgotten the presence of God in their relationship. Rather than augmenting the relationship, this diminishes its greatness.

In sharp contrast to the special relationship, a "holy relationship" rests on solid ground. Each partner has looked within himself and perceives nothing inherent lacking. Accepting his own completion, he finds pleasure in extending it, and so joins with another person who is also whole. Because they've both evolved to the same degree, no great differences exist between them. This relationship contains and reflects heaven's holiness.

Completion comes from union with God, and from the extension of that union to others. As such, a holy partnership mirrors the rich relationship between the Son of God and his Father; it has the power to alleviate all suffering. In such a partnership, sin cannot exist, since God himself has arranged each holy union in accordance with His own plan.

A holy relationship requires that both partners strive together toward a common goal. When two people share the same intent and they search for the love of God, a healing takes place. Giving flows endlessly. No wants or needs hinder it, for in giving of themselves, both are blessed. Moreover, these blessings flourish and extend to others. A light emanates outward, illuminating the world. In a holy relationship, seemingly difficult situations are accepted as blessings. Instead of obsessively criticizing one's partner, forever pointing out any imperfections that must be changed or discarded, there is a pull toward praise and appreciation. Having created an atmosphere of love, each partner may begin to perceive the Christ in each other.

A Course in Miracles
on Relationships

The concept of the Sonship must be counted as one of the most important ideas presented in *A Course in Miracles*. The Sonship is made up of all God's children, meaning Jesus and all humankind. Its wholeness and integrity provide a solid foundation for world peace:

> It should especially be noted that God has only one Son. If all His creations are His Sons, every one must be an integral part of the whole Sonship. The Sonship in its oneness transcends the sum of its parts . . . conflict cannot ultimately be resolved until all the parts of the Sonship have returned. (Text, p. 29)

The *Course*'s narrator, presumed to be Jesus, warns us to avoid separation from our brothers. In appreciating one another, we honor the Holy Spirit most deeply:

> You cannot understand yourself alone. This is because you have no meaning apart from your rightful place in the Sonship, and rightful place of the Sonship is God. (Text, p. 73)

Your gratitude to your brother is the only gift I want. I will bring it to God for you, knowing that to know your brother is to know God. If you are grateful to your brother, you are grateful to God for what He created. Through your gratitude you come to know your brother, and one moment of real recognition makes everyone your brother because each of them is of your Father. (Text, p. 63)

Ironically, when crises destabilize our lives—just when we most need each other's support—we often feel a strange inner "pull," separating us from friends and acquaintances. But disassociation is no solution; it is a delusion (paraphrase, Text, p. 136). The *Course* teaches us:

Alone we can do nothing, but together our minds fuse into something whose power is far beyond the power of its separate parts. (Text, p. 136)

Our function is to work together, because apart from each other we cannot function at all. The power of God's Son lies in all of us, but not in any of us alone. . . . Whom God has joined cannot be separated, and God has joined all His Sons with Himself. (Text, p. 139)

You cannot enter God's presence . . . alone. . . . All your brothers must enter with you, for until you have accepted them you cannot enter. For you cannot understand Wholeness unless you are whole. (Text, p. 185, 186)

You must recognize your brother as your savior and friend, with whom you will travel to paradise:

> Give joyously to one another the freedom and the strength to lead you there. And come before each other's holy altar where the strength and freedom wait, to offer and receive the bright awareness that leads you home. The lamp is lit in both of you for one another. And by the hands that gave it to your brother shall both of you be led past fear to love. (Text, p. 399)

Only your brother holds the power to forgive your errors. And he, in turn, must seek forgiveness from someone other than *himself*. No one of us can forgive ourselves alone:

> Beside each of you is one who offers you the chance of Atonement, for the Holy Spirit is on him. Would you hold his sins against him, or accept his gift to you? Is this giver of salvation your friend or enemy? Choose which he is, remembering that you will receive of him according to your choice.
>
> There is no grace of Heaven that you cannot offer to one another, and receive from your most holy Friend. . . . Think who your brother is, before you would condemn him. And offer thanks to God that he is holy. . . . Join him in gladness, and remove all trace of guilt from his disturbed and tortured mind. . . . Give faith to one another for faith and hope and mercy are yours to give. Into the hands that give, the gift is given. (Text, p. 394)

It is not our job, the *Course* explains, to change our brother, but to accept him as he is, for *"his errors do not come from the truth that is him."* (Text, p. 156) We need to take a good look at where we invest our valuable energy. When we react to our brother's errors as if they are real, we actually *make* them a reality. In confirming that our brother's sins are real, we condemn ourselves—for all of us comprise the Sonship.

When we accept our brother *unconditionally*, on the other hand, we open the door to loving all of humanity. Yet acceptance doesn't mean a mere absence of condemnation. For *correction*, however well intended, can also become a form of attack:

> The choice to judge rather than to know is the cause of the loss of peace. . . . You have no idea of the tremendous release and deep peace that comes from meeting yourself and your brothers totally without judgment. In the presence of knowledge all judgment is automatically suspended. (Text, p. 42)

> When you correct a brother you are telling him that he is wrong. He may be making no sense at the time, and it is certain that, if he is speaking from the ego, he will not be making sense. But your task is to still tell him he is right. . . . He is still right, because he is a Son of God. . . . If you point out the errors of your brother's ego you must be seeing through yours, because the Holy Spirit does not perceive his errors . . . nothing the ego makes means anything. . . . When a brother behaves insanely, you can heal him only by perceiving the sanity in him. (Text, p. 155)

According to the *Course*, all conflict arises from the ego, for *only the Holy Spirit is conflict-free* (Text, p. 91):

> . . . the ego perceives itself at war and therefore in need of allies. You who are not at war must look for brothers and recognize all whom you see as brothers, because only equals are at peace. Because God's equal Sons have everything, they cannot compete. Yet if they perceive any of their brothers as anything other than their perfect equals, the idea of competition has entered their minds. (Text, p. 108)

> Every response to the ego is a call to war—Those whom you perceive as opponents are part of your peace, which you are giving up by attacking them. . . . When you give up peace, you are excluding yourself from it. (Text, p. 128)

Let's consider the major causes of conflict: guilt and blame. Where do these originate? Are they real or imagined? The *Course* explains that guilt and blame arise from the same source—the ego—and that neither has any place in the realm of the infinite:

> The ego tells you all is black with guilt within you, and bids you not to look. Instead, it bids you look upon your brothers, and see the guilt in them. (Text, p. 244)

> If your brothers are part of you and you blame them for your deprivation, you are blaming yourself. And you cannot blame yourself without blaming them. (Text, p. 187)

If God knows His Children as wholly sinless, it is blasphemous to perceive them as guilty. (Text, p. 178)

The ego expresses itself in both overt and less obvious ways. Though we may be aware of how the ego drives us to attack or to cause conflict, we're often "in the dark" when it comes to recognizing the ego's more insidious role as the mastermind of our *projections*. What are projections, and how do they work? When we project, we unconsciously displace all of our *own* feelings—our fears, anger, love, disgust, disinterest—onto another person. We come to believe quite sincerely that the *other person really has these feelings, instead of ourselves:*

> ... the ego is incapable of trust. ... It believes that your brothers ... are out to take God from you. Whenever a brother attacks another, that is what he believes. Projection always sees your wishes in others. If you choose to separate yourself from God, that is what you will think others are doing to you. (Text, p. 119)

As you know, mistakenly attributing feelings to your partner can only cause havoc in a relationship:

> The ego cannot tolerate release from the past. ... It dictates your reactions to those you meet in the present from a past reference point, obscuring the present reality ... you will then react to your brother as though he were someone else, and this will surely prevent you from recognizing him as he is [now]. (Text, p. 229)

. . . To perceive truly is to . . . perceive a brother only as you can see him now. His past has no reality in the present. (Text, p. 233)

Letting go of the past and all projections associated with it is no small feat. It requires an act of faith—and *faith* is exactly what *A Course in Miracles* urges us to act upon. Faith, we are told, is the only road to peace:

> Believe in your brothers because I believe in you, and you will learn that my belief in you is justified. Believe in me by believing in them, for the sake of what God gave them. Do not ask for blessings without blessing them. (Text, p. 154)

> When you accepted trust as the goal for your relationship, you became a giver of peace as surely as your Father gave peace to you. For the goal of peace cannot be accepted apart from its conditions. (Text, p. 346)

As all ancient spiritual scriptures attest, we will have to overcome great obstacles along the road to peace. The greatest of these is the ego. As it tries to obscure our path, the ego plays games not only with the mind and the spirit, but also with our flesh. As we travel down this road, we may be pulled in two directions. While the Holy Spirit guides us to use our bodies solely to reach out to our brothers to *connect* with one another, the ego uses our bodies to *separate* us, by encouraging us to attack our brothers:

> The Holy Spirit reaches through [the body] to others. You do not perceive your brothers as the Holy Spirit does, because you do not

regard bodies solely as a means of joining minds and uniting them with yours and mine. . . . If you use the body for attack, it is harmful to you. . . . Communication ends separation. Attack promotes it. (Text, p. 140)

Remember that those who attack are poor. (Text, p. 205) If you will recognize that all the attack you perceive is in your mind and nowhere else, you will at last have placed its source and where it begins it must end. (Text, p. 207)

You have no enemy except yourself. . . . beware of the temptation to perceive yourself unfairly treated. (Text, p. 523)

The strong do not attack because they see no need to do so. Before the idea of attack can enter your mind, you must have perceived yourself as weak. . . . No longer perceiving yourself and your brothers as equal, and regarding yourself as weaker, you attempt to "equalize" the situation you made. (Text, p. 209)

But what should we do when another person's actions have harmed us—have we no right to blame him? *A Course in Miracles* answers this question in a surprising way. *"When a brother acts insanely,"* it says, he actually offers us *an opportunity to bless him.* (Text, p. 118). In this way, his needs lay bare our *own*, for we also *need the blessing we can give* (paraphrase, Text, p. 118).

There is no way . . . to have it except by giving it. This is the law of God, and it has no exceptions. (Text, p. 118)

We must exempt no one from the love we feel, or we will be hiding a dark place in [our] mind where the Holy Spirit is not welcome. (Text, p. 227)

How far should we go in reaching out to another? What good will it do for us to keep trying, when we see no possible solution to our brother's problem?

The Bible says that you should go with a brother twice as far as he asks. Devotion to a brother cannot set you back either. . . . It can lead only to mutual progress. The result of genuine devotion is inspiration, a word which properly understood is the opposite of fatigue. (Text, p. 47)

It is impossible to overestimate your brother's value. . . . It will be given you to see your brother's worth when all you want for him is peace. And what you want for him you will receive. (Text, p. 405)

Love's path steadily weaves its way through every paragraph of *A Course in Miracles*. Without a doubt, the commitment to love is the *Course*'s most precious gift to us, and the text's central theme:

Every loving thought is true. Everything else is an appeal for healing and help, regardless of the form it takes. Can anyone be justified in responding with anger to a brother's plea for help? No response can be appropriate except the willingness to give it to him, for this and only this is what he is asking for. (Text, p. 200)

When you meet anyone, remember that it is a holy encounter. As you see him you will see yourself. As you treat him you will treat yourself. As you think of him, you will think of yourself. Never forget this. . . . Whenever two Sons of God meet, they are given another chance at salvation. (Text, p. 132)

Only appreciation is an appropriate response to your brother. Gratitude is due him for both his loving thoughts and his appeal for help, for both are capable of bringing love into your awareness if you perceive them truly. (Text, p. 201)

Give them the appreciation God accords them always, because they are His beloved Son in whom He is well pleased. You cannot be apart from them because you are not apart from Him. . . . You cannot know your own perfection until you have honored all those who were created like you. (Text, p. 119)

When your relationships are free of blame, no one can harm you. If your center is intact and your heart with God, you'll be able to adjust to even the most sudden and fundamental change.

You cannot be hurt, and do not want to show your brother anything except your wholeness. Show him that he cannot hurt you and hold nothing against him, or you hold it against yourself. This is the meaning of 'turning the other cheek.' (Text, p. 75)

Overlooking our brother's errors doesn't mean going away wounded and resentful. We must not separate ourselves from him. Taking his arm, we must walk together with him. In this way, we become closer to him still:

By following [the Holy Spirit] you are led back to God where you belong, and how can you find the way except by taking your brother with you? . . . You forsake yourself and God if you forsake any of your brothers. You must learn to see them as they are, and understand they belong to God as you do. (Text, p. 76)

All my brothers are special. If they believe that they are deprived of anything, their perception becomes distorted. When this occurs the whole family of God or the Sonship is impaired in its relationships. . . . God is not partial. All His children have His total Love, and all His gifts are freely given to everyone alike.

The fact that each one has this power completely is a condition entirely alien to the world's thinking. The world believes that if anyone has everything there is nothing left. (Text, p. 41)

Isn't it beautiful that *all* of us *can* really *have everything*—that we can all have our power *completely*, all at the same time? Imagine if everyone in the world understood this! Imagine how it would be if in sharing what we possess we would *lose nothing*. Sharing would simply become an act of love, in no way a threat to our own resources:

The way to recognize your brother is by recognizing the Holy Spirit in him . . . the idea of the Holy Spirit is . . . strengthened by being given away. It increases as you give it to your brother. Your brother does not even have to be aware of the Holy Spirit in himself or in you for this miracle to occur. . . . See him through the Holy

Spirit in his mind, and you will recognize Him in yours. What you acknowledge in your brother you are acknowledging in yourself and what you share you strengthen. (Text, p. 72)

Nothing real can be increased except by sharing. That is why God created you. (Text, p. 64)

The Christ-like voice that dictated *A Course in Miracles* insists that loving our brothers, loving the Holy Spirit, and loving ourselves is *one and the same*. No teaching can be more effective in changing the world:

Recognizing the Majesty of God as your brother is to accept your own inheritance. God gives only equally. If you recognize His gift in any-one, you have acknowledged what He has given you. (Text, p. 127)

As you come closer to a brother you approach me, and as you with-draw from him I become distant to you. Salvation is a collaborative venture. It cannot be undertaken successfully by those who disen-gage themselves from the Sonship, because they are disengaging themselves from me. God will come to you only as you will give Him to your brothers. Learn first of them and you will be ready to hear God. That is because the function of Love is one. (Text, p. 63)

INTIMACY WITH EVERYONE

Notice how you felt when you read "Intimacy with Everyone." Most people react by exclaiming, "Oh, my God, is she recommending sex with everyone?" No, I'm not. I'm recommending intimacy—emotional and spiritual intimacy.

A Course in Miracles teaches us that if you love only parts of reality, you don't know what love means. If you love unlike God, who knows no special love, how can you understand it? As Children of God, all human beings together comprise the Sonship. By desiring a special relationship with only one other human being, we limit our love to only one small segment of the Sonship. Somewhere inside us we intuitively know we have forsaken the totality of the Sonship. This knowledge creates guilt in our minds and our relationships. Guilt houses fear; love where fear has entered is not perfect.

God is not partial, so why are we? If we develop our consciousness to the level required, we can be in love with everyone. That is what the spiritual master does. He falls in love with everyone. In an enlightened relationship, loving everyone isn't a threat to either partner because each understands that the Holy Spirit is in everyone. In a Community of Majesty, intimacy with everyone occurs naturally. Jealousy and sibling rivalry are addressed and dealt with openly.

Most people, even enlightened beings who are in a committed relationship, prefer monogamy. Having an outside sexual relationship would dilute the significance of their relationship and be a distraction. It is logical that if a person wants to have an open relationship, he or she should find someone else who also wants, or can tolerate, that model. Different cultures vary somewhat as regards monogamy. In Europe, it seems to be more acceptable to have open affairs. Secret affairs usually don't turn out well anywhere in the world simply because their conception is without integrity (being hidden), and the subsequent subconscious guilt creates havoc, pain, and more bad karma. Some people think they want several open sexual relationships at once. But they often find such a situation too complicated to be practical.

Affairs often start because a couple's intimate life becomes neglected. It has often been said that women crave intimacy and men avoid it. Often men who are described by women as "emotionally crippled" will even defend their emotional unavailability as "normal"! A woman who is used to intimacy might try to force it upon a man. Psychologist Helen Formaini believes that men actually see danger in affiliation and safety in isolation. They fear women as they fear self-knowledge. This will change as we move into male-female balance in the New Paradigm.

What if everyone (men and women) has some fear of intimacy? If we deny ourselves this opportunity for self-knowledge, how can we fully develop our capacity for love and tenderness? Fear of intimacy isn't just a personal shortcoming; it is very bad for our health and can lead to tragic consequences. We need to stop protecting ourselves from hurt and develop the emotional courage to take the risk of staying open.

A Community of Majesty

Imagine belonging to a group of fabulous people who are working on enlightened projects together and helping each other to become healed, happy, and whole. I'm not talking about belonging to a commune. I'm not talking about joining a cult. Quite the opposite. In fact, my book *Pure Joy* includes an essay called "The Difference Between a Cult and a True Spiritual Family." I'm talking about a support system.

I envision a paradigm in which you and your mate are part of a supportive group of people who understand who you are and who empower you both to become all that you can be. A community where you can sincerely and openly share the problems you're having in your relationship or in your life and get help with them. It's very important to belong to a spiritual family when you're moving into new paradigms and breaking with cultural tradition. Otherwise, you'll feel alone, as if it's you against the world. A great deal of pressure is taken off your relationship when you have friends you feel intimately close with who nurture you.

Imagine hanging out with a group of individuals who are totally alive, safe, peaceful, innocent, present, and experiencing their own magnificence. Imagine spending time with future "super-beings" who maintain perfect health and even prevent aging and death! Do you question your qualifications? Well, if you're reading this book, your higher self already knows what is good for you and who you are and what you can be. It's only a question of acting upon this knowledge.

Imagine being with those who experience natural abundance and who want you to experience abundance as well. Imagine people who actually express their Christ-nature! Imagine going to this group and finding a mate if you want one. Imagine being highly productive in such energy. Imagine working with this group on important planetary issues and getting involved in local solutions for your community. Imagine the celebration of having such friends! This is already happening. We have communities of Immortals in many cities of the world already. In fact, if you travel to Paris, London, Madrid, Milan, Los Angeles, and many other places, you can contact them. Call the Rebirthing community for information.

We lovingly call this family the *Ohana*. This is a Hawaiian word which means "extended family" or "chosen family who breathes together." ("Ha" means "breath" in the Hawaiian language.) This family is dedicated to life itself. I am now introducing the Divine Mother Movement into these communities in order to achieve a higher rebirthing rate.

If rebirthing has not begun in your area, we can bring it to you, right to your doorstep. You gather your friends together and we send a speaker who can train you in the art and science of rebirthing. We can tech you the knowledge of Physical Immortality. We can teach you "Relationships technology" and bring the relationships seminars to your community. We invite you to join us. We look forward to knowing you.

A LIFE OF SERVICE

The reason human beings don't have self-illumination and continuous joy is because of their *samskaras* or the accumulated imprints of past experience. Samskaras should be entirely removed for total liberation. It is important to understand the law of karma (i.e., you reap what you sow, what you do to another is also done to you). Traditionally, great beings remove samskaras by renunciation, solitude, fasting, penance, and by desiring nothing. However, living the life of a complete ascetic can be counterproductive to a relationship. The masters say that you can begin to alleviate conflict by replacing lower values with higher ones. Also, it is recommended that you sublimate your energy into spiritual channels through meditation, devotion, and selfless service.

My master Babaji encourages us to live a life of truth, simplicity, love, service to mankind, and Karma Yoga (work dedicated to God and humanity). He tells us that Karma Yoga is the highest yoga and that it can change our fate. He tells us that idleness is death. Work is worship. Dedicate all of your work to God every day. This will change your life for the better.

The only danger in dedicating your life to serving society (such as charity work) is having a false motive. If you do it for recognition, pride, or for making someone obligated to you, you can do harm to others and yourself by creating more samskaras. Selfless service means that you're willing to give up personal motives. It is also necessary to have spiritual understanding. For example, you might decide to feed the poor. This can be really wonderful. However, a beggar of food may be creating his own samskaras and you may be inadvertently binding him tighter to his pattern. Cultivating his intellect and raising his self-esteem (so he can return to work) is more helpful because it's contrary to his pattern. In other words, some service can be a disservice.

Serving a sick person's bodily needs and helping her get back on her feet is a valuable service. Anything that you can do to uplift and advance humanity is good service. Remember, it should always come from the outpouring of your being.

When my husband and I joined the Peace Corps, we were touched more deeply by this experience than anything else in our lives. I consider that time to be the "boot camp" that helped me leap into world service. We were happier then than at any other time in our marriage because we had nothing but our love and the purest kind of work—service without pay.

Money is important, but you must remember the difference between need and desire. You don't always need what you want. Meher Baba once said that *wanting is a source of perpetual restlessness*. If you don't get what you want, you're disappointed. If you get it, you want more. Watch out!

I honor Babaji and Meher Baba for inspiring me to write this essay. One thing I've noticed about my spiritual masters is this: They are in bliss. They all serve selflessly and institute projects of incredible value, such as free schools for the poor. Decide which contributions you and your mate will make. Don't be tied to results, but stick to it no matter the outcome.

ADVANCED SPIRITUAL DYNAMICS IN RELATIONSHIPS

CHAPTER 11

The Whole Woman understands that she is not her ego and is clear that she is one with God. The Whole Woman understands that she is an aspect of the Divine Mother and is loving, nurturing, giving, compassionate, and wonderful.

In India, all great gurus surrender to and worship the Divine Mother. If men from other parts of the world traveled there and saw this embodiment of real power, they would reevaluate their ideas of what power can be. Yogananda once said, "Every man who looks upon women as an incarnation of the Divine Mother will find salvation." When you do this, universal love will come into your heart, and you will draw from women many spiritual gifts.

You must surrender the self to the Divine Self. We suffer only because we identify with our ego rather than with our True Reality, or Spirit. To find real life, we must die the death of the ego to be reborn spiritually. Give yourself up to God completely. *A Course in*

Miracles says, "Only an illusion stands between you and the holy Self that you are." In a spiritual relationship, we should assist each other in this goal of self-surrender.

Early in a relationship, you can tell your mate about the issues you're working on at the time, including the ultimate one of self-surrender. You can ask for his support and promise to work on your problem with diligence. You give your mate permission to point out your unconscious backsliding; you are grateful to be awakened about it. This is the level of trust needed for honest feedback. It begins with fearless self-analysis to stand the critique of others without flinching.

You first have to ask yourself: Are you afraid of losing control or of being controlled by others? If so, this will be triggered the minute someone assumes a role remotely resembling a parent or authority figure. It comes down to letting go of ego control and accepting that the Divine runs everything. If two people can stay out of control together, it is bliss. It is ecstasy. This requires that both totally surrender to Divine Control.

Love is the highest energy known to man, but we tend to make the love of a man or woman our ultimate goal. We become blind to the real goal of life which is to become intoxicated with Divine Love. Human love can gradually be transmuted to Divine Love, but only when a person or a couple attain spiritual perfection. Always remember that behind all human love is the spiritual love of God. Yogananda calls it "the romance of Divine Love."

The highest reality is that you and your mate are one with God. Everything else just isn't real. Everything else is but a representation of only an aspect of the ego. The ego is a mistaken identity, a false self that we create.

The ego is the thought that we are separate from God, but we cannot be separate from God. You can dispel this illusion by withdrawing your belief in it. The allegiance to it is what gives it power.

All the purifications and spiritual processes I recommend are for clearing this persistent veil of illusion. Relationships of any kind help this process.

THE WHOLE WOMAN

The Whole Woman knows who she is. She is clear that she is one with God. She is enlightened and therefore she is aware that her own thoughts produce her own results. She is not a victim and she does not blame men or anyone else. She is not angry at men or anyone else. She does not feel limited as a woman. She understands that she is not her ego, which is limitation itself. She lives in terms of her being, instead of in terms of pleasing. She is true to her essence and her spiritual path, always.

The Whole Woman honors and trusts her intuition. She can express her intuitive ideas in such a way that others are excited to hear them. She does not have to push or manipulate. She simply has enough self-esteem to express her intuitive ideas so that they are heard and appreciated. She doesn't feel held back by men because she doesn't allow them to hold her back. Her position is natural and non-threatening because it comes from her heart and her spirituality.

The Whole Woman holds her feminine and masculine sides in balance. She can easily stand up for herself, and she is not afraid to be seen *and* heard. She can express her opinions fully and without hesitation. She enjoys being female and is totally comfortable with her sexuality.

The Whole Woman understands that she is an aspect of the Divine Mother. She knows she isn't a sex object. She is loving, soft, nurturing, giving, compassionate, caring, vulnerable, and wonderful. She is also strong and productive and always searches for the truth. Cooperativeness and peacefulness do not make her weak. She has high self-esteem and respect for herself always, whether she is at home with the children, in the workplace, or involved with both.

The Whole Woman will not sell out just to keep the peace. She will not tolerate sexism, male superiority, or sarcasm. But she does love men. She is not against them. Her goal is to raise the consciousness of herself, her loved ones, and all of society. She understands that she is capable of producing positive change on the planet. The Whole Woman is not afraid of her power; she doesn't feel that she is a threat to men. She attracts men who like and are excited by her wholeness and spirituality. She knows that her intelligence, love, spirituality, and sexuality are wonderful qualities and will attract wonderful people. She knows her feminine qualities are appreciated by all.

The Whole Woman is healthy because her mind is pure, and she is an overflowing spring of aliveness. She is full of her magnificence and, because it is simply the truth, she displays no arrogance. She is all of these things whether or not she is with a man. She is all of these things whether or not she is a mother. She doesn't invalidate herself, because she understands her own value. The Whole Woman is someone people want to be with! She is an asset to all. The more total she is, the deeper she can enter into her relationships; and the more intimacy she can sustain. The Whole Woman is not overwhelming. She is fun to be with! She is worth waiting for.

ESPECIALLY FOR MEN

In India, all the great gurus, sadhus, and immortal Yogis (who are the most powerful men I've ever met) surrender to and worship the Divine Mother. If you could travel to India with me to meet them, and *see* this real power for yourself, you would reevaluate your idea of power. I honestly think you would want to be like them. And it's never too late for you to become a spiritual master. I salute any man reading this. Bless you. Where are you? Please let us know!

The spiritual master Yogananda said, "Every man who looks upon woman as an incarnation of the Divine Mother will find salvation." I think he meant that when you do this, as the God-realized masters have always done, universal love will come into your heart and you will be able to draw from women many spiritual treasures.

The most fabulous women I know are just craving liberated men. Women simply want to create their independence out of internal security; they don't *want* to fight with you.

In fact, we women want to co-create with you in a way that also excites you! We don't want your real self to be different. We just want our relationship to change so we can also accept our spiritual responsibility for the planet—alongside you. We would like to work out a New Paradigm with you. Historically, there have been societies where women were honored and had very respected positions. They weren't only honored as priestesses and oracles, they were included in leadership and there was true equality. It is starting to happen again—it is inevitable. Soon, the new definition of power will include being able to handle an equal relationship! You can be sure of it. So why not start now? The paradigm of men and women as equals running society together is not only spiritually appropriate; it is also a "turn on."

We would like to see more of you in seminars. They are great places to meet great women. Maybe that sounds corny, but I mean it in the sincerest sense. Socializing shouldn't be the main purpose of a seminar, but it is a wonderful benefit.

Soon we will all become sick of the imbalance of power we see daily. Envy and hatred will become so bad we simply won't be able to tolerate it. Aren't we tired of suffering NOW? We all co-created this situation. If we can learn to work together, be on the same side, we will all be winners; the children of the world will be winners, too. Supporting equal rights for women can release bad karma!

After I wrote this essay, a friend called to say that her spiritual teacher had just told her that he is working with more women now because "women are the way for men to come home." He was talking about our real home, of course, going back to the Divine Mother and merging with the higher love, the pure love, the Divine Love. It is through this Divine Love that we will, together, be able to tune into the Divine Plan for Humanity. The Divine Mother will teach us cooperation.

SURRENDER

When you hear the word "surrender," you might imagine having to give in to someone else's wishers or demands. But what I am actually referring to is a surrender of self—a surrender to one's Divine Self. We suffer only because we're ignorant of our true being, because we believe that we are our ego. We are ignorant because we identify with our Ego Mind, body, and physical senses rather than with our True Reality, or Spirit (Atman). As long as we maintain this ignorance, we forget that God is within us and we feel empty. We want to find a substitute to feel full again, and we don't know what. We start craving things. We accumulate desires and try out everything to find what we're seeking. We continue wanting something. This continuous craving and its related action involves us in even more binding karmas. Soon, we end up craving death!

To find real life, we must transcend the ego. The ego is the barrier to happiness and knowledge. You have to die the death of the ego to be reborn spiritually. This is the major obstacle to overcome in spiritual life, whether you're Christian, Hindu, or Buddhist. The ego is the only obstacle to God Consciousness. So, what do you have to do? Surrender yourself. Give yourself up to God completely. Become absorbed in God. It sounds simple, but it is one of the hardest tasks one can possibly undertake. You have to be vigilant against the ego. God is the only reality. You have to know in your heart that God not only exists, but is attainable as well. You won't reach God by leaving the world. You get there by surrendering your ego to God every moment of your life.

In a relationship, we should assist each other in this goal of self-surrender. The problem is that "truth cannot deal with errors that you want." In other words, your mate, your teacher, or anyone else may want to help you see the truth, but if you don't let go of your ego's false beliefs, then nobody can help you.

Everyone who is open to a New Paradigm must first deal with an identity problem. Example: If you think you're separate from God, you will feel weak, you will have fear, and you will have low self-esteem. The *Course* says, "Every decision you make stems from what you think you are, and represents the value you place on yourself. Only an illusion stands between you and the holy Self that you are." The ego must be replaced by the truth, which knows no separateness.

The *Course* says that in you is all of heaven. All power is given unto you in earth and heaven; there is nothing that you cannot do. When you join with another in a holy relationship, you join in truth and relinquish the belief that your identity is ego. When truth is the goal of your relationship, you become a giver of peace.

Encouragement and Gratitude

There is nothing new about the qualities of encouragement and gratitude; but there may be a new way to use them in an enlightened relationship. Imagine this:

Early in a relationship, you tell your mate about the issues you're working on at this time in your life. You ask your mate for his or her support and encouragement with this problem. You also promise to work on your problem with diligence. You are grateful for your mate's support. You don't feel threatened. You express this gratitude when you're getting encouragement and support. You also give your mate permission to point out your unconscious backsliding; furthermore, you're grateful to be awakened about it. Your mate always tries to be encouraging rather than critical by holding the thought that this block can be healed.

Sound impossible? Well, it isn't. This is happening more and more in our communities. In the beginning, we made mistakes. We were often at the mercy of our blind spots. We knew we needed feedback but we were still sometimes defensive about receiving it—and often critical in giving it. But we never abandoned the model, and it's improving all the time. We've learned that if you can analyze yourself fearlessly, you can stand the critical analysis of others without flinching. Also, by not being defensive, feedback comes to you much more diplomatically and tenderly, with encouragement. Defenses attract attack. Both of these lessons became evident simultaneously. By the time we mastered self-analysis, and it no longer mattered how someone expressed feedback, the wording had become much more encouraging anyway.

The level reached by those of us who have stuck with this process is best described as a keen awareness of our "hang-ups"—and we do ask our mates and the community for support in coping with them. We are grateful. If we don't recognize our faults and someone else points them out to us, we're even more grateful. We want to know how we're coming across. Try this attitude. Start now!

The old way of handling each other's faults has been called "co-dependent bargaining." A couple had an unconscious "agreement" which went something like this: "I won't confront your heavy smoking habit, if you won't make me confront my spending habits." There is mutual denial—no attempt on either side to encourage soul progress. In the New Paradigm, there is no tolerance for co-dependent maneuvers that only leave you more stuck. The opposite of denial would be overkill (or dwelling too much) on your mate's faults. There should be an appropriate balance. Self-analysis is the key. Remember this quote from Yogananda: "Those who DWELL on faults of others are like human vultures" (Yogananda, 1982). Practice encouragement. Everyone will consider you a friend, a helper.

I've been trying a new approach in my personal life. I try, as soon as I can, to have the *most* gratitude for what upsets me the most about a companion. Upsets reveal shadows I need to look for in myself.

DIVINE CONTROL

Are you afraid of losing control or of being controlled by others? If so, you can be sure you will attract it. You will find somebody to control you so you can, in turn, resent it. You will imagine that you're being controlled the minute someone assumes a role remotely resembling a parent or authority figure. Let's examine the real question of control.

If you're out of control, then nobody can control you. If you're in control, then you're using your ego to stop the flow of life, or the Holy Spirit, from roaring through you. In this sense, you're using the Ego Mind against yourself, which causes pain, sickness, accident, or even death. In rebirthing, if you stop the life force by hanging onto a negative thought with power, you experience paralysis. People believe that, if they let go, something terrible will happen. But all that you really let go of is negative thoughts that would hurt you otherwise. If you can let go of ego control, and accept that the Divine runs everything, then you will experience an abundance of life, energy, love, joy, and money!

When you meet a true guru, you don't think about controlling him or her. You want to surrender instead. A true guru, male or female, is totally guided by Divine Control. He or she is completely in present time—completely there with you—completely conscious, alive, wild, and connected to everything. This person is "God-intoxicated" and irresistible. You want to surrender and you want to be like them. Often, you cannot tolerate staying in a guru's presence very long if you do not surrender. You confront your own unwillingness to be in present time, your own limitations, your own blocks and negative addictions. So you stay as long as you can without going crazy. Later, you return for more teaching and insight, hoping to be more like your guru the next time. The guru teaches you Divine Control.

If two people can stay out of control together, it is bliss. It is ecstasy. Staying out of control requires that both totally surrender to Divine Control by giving up their ego-based addictions. This rarely happens at the same time, and when it does, it is mostly during sexual ecstasy; that is why people are addicted to sex. But what if you could be out of control *all of the time?* It is something to pray for. It is your goal in the New Paradigm.

Controlling someone with the use of anger or fear is not only manipulative, it misses the point spiritually. Manipulation, control, and anger aren't the exercise of true power, which is love, safety, and certainty. Someone who is certain about their identity, and who is completely loving and safe, can walk into a room and take control without even speaking. He or she doesn't need to control anything, they just are and that is enough. If you have met a saint like this, you're very fortunate.

DIVINE LOVE

Plato saw love as a ladder consisting of seven steps ranging from love of an individual to love of the universe's highest realities. The bottom step is number one, as follows:

1. Falling in love with the quality of another's form.
2. Loving all beautiful, physical forms.
3. Loving the beauty of the mind, regardless of form.
4. Loving beautiful practices, such as ethics, fairness, justice, and kindness.
5. Developing a love of beautiful institutions such as family and society.
6. Developing a love of the universal and the abstract including the sciences, loving the whole cosmos.
7. Experiencing a love of the everlasting manifestation of beauty itself: The immortal Absolute.

Love is the highest energy known to man. Love and life itself are one. *A Course in Miracles* would say that we don't have to seek love; we just have to remove blocks to the awareness of love's existence. We have to dismantle the blocks we've built against love.

We tend to make the love of a man or a woman our ultimate goal in life—that is very limiting. We are blind to the real goal of life, which is to become intoxicated with Divine Love. Human love has the potential to be gradually transmuted to Divine Love. Relationships experienced only through the body can only end up in disaster and misery. They become what the *Course* calls "special hate relationships." Human love manifests itself at different levels depending on how entrenched one's ego is. The lower forms of love can easily turn into hate. Meher Baba said that the lowest forms of love (i.e., infatuation, lust, and greed) are actually perverted forms of loving. But even the highest form of human love differs qualitatively from Divine Love.

Divine Love blooms when a person attains spiritual perfection. Divine Love can descend upon a human being by the grace of a perfect master or the Divine Mother herself when this being has been prepared spiritually. Supreme Divine Love arises once the individual human Ego Mind disappears. This occurs after lifetimes of spiritual purification or when the Perfect Master determines that the aspirant is ready. When Divine Love is present, the person is God-intoxicated and irresistible. Shastriji manifests this state at all times. He possesses unbounded spontaneity. Divine Love is God. It is still possible to meet him!

The great masters in history were channelers of Divine Love. Think of Jesus. Think of Buddha. Babaji. They're our true models. The goal of every being must be Divine Love. It isn't reserved for just a few. It's the ultimate destiny of all souls. Always remember that behind all human love is the spiritual love of God. Yogananda calls it "the romance of Divine Love"

(Yogananda, 1982). The greatest romance is with the Infinite. If you're living with someone, seek the Divine together. Ask the Cosmic Divine Mother to purify you so that you can channel this Divine Love daily, and with deepest sincerity.

THE HIGHEST REALITY

The highest reality is that you are one with God, and your mate is one with God. God is life and love and bliss. Everything else isn't real. Everything else is an illusion. Everything else is only an aspect of the ego and the ego is merely a fearful thought, a mistaken identity, a false self we create. The ego is the thought that you're separate from God. But you cannot really be separate from God.

Belief in the ego, however, causes you to experience separation; it makes you experience fear, guilt, pain, misery, struggle, conflict, worry, disease, depression, and death. The ego is just a belief. You can dispel its illusion by withdrawing your belief in it. It is only your allegiance to it that gives it any power.

When your mate is experiencing his limited mind (ego states listed above), you must be careful not to agree with his illusion about himself. See your mate as healed. See your mate as perfect, alive, loving, joyful, peaceful, and immortal (the Holy Spirit's mind). This is precisely how Jesus healed people: He refused to accept their limited mind. He saw only the Holy Spirit in them; his reality was so clear and strong that, in his presence, people couldn't maintain their old reality.

However, when your mate is having a crisis, he believes it is real. He experiences fear, because the ego is fear and the fear seems real. We are addicted to our belief in the ego, and waking up to reality takes time. So it's best to allow your mate to feel and to express and not cut him off. Gently remind your partner who he really is and what he really can do. This is the encouragement he needs. Encourage your mate to remember the Holy Spirit's mind.

As for all of the purifications and spiritual processes recommended in this book, their only purpose is for clearing away the veils of illusion which, in fact, are just cobwebs that cover up the real self—the God-realized Self. Having a relationship of any kind helps this process. "No one alone can judge the ego truly. Yet when two or more join together in searching for Truth, the ego can no longer defend its lack of content. Our union is therefore the way to renounce the ego in you. The truth is both of us is beyond the ego" (Vaughan and Walsh, 1992).

To understand the Highest Reality to the fullest, read *A Course in Miracles* completely. If you find it too difficult at first, you can refer to the study guide I've prepared called *Drinking the Divine*. This essay is a small step toward understanding the *Course*, which is the real truth. If we could all stay in that paradigm, which is our true reality already, we would not need this book or any other book; there would be no conflict in relationships.

However, until we reintegrate who we really are, we will have to do the best with where we are now. In the meantime, we can invite the Holy Spirit into our minds for correction of all our wrong thinking, and pray that our relationship be used for His purpose.

APPENDIX

THE IMMORTAL RELATIONSHIP

The unconscious death urge originated eons ago when we decided we were separate from God. All disharmony stems from this separation. Most people slowly kill themselves, and by extension their relationship, by thinking that "death is inevitable." Thus, every couple must go through what we call the "death urge of the relationship" sooner or later. This belief is the outgrowth of religious and societal programming and can be addressed by identifying "anti-life" thinking and clearing it, individually and as a couple.

Its counter is the concept and the goal of physical immortality. Most people feel unsettled by the idea of living forever, since it differs markedly from the "life after death" concept of most religions. *A Course in Miracles* says life springs from "a thought called God," so increasing the sacred life force within us through joy, right thinking, and right action is actually what the Bible called "overcoming"—death is conquered through the exaltation of love, praise, and gratitude, but in this life not the next.

Many people will say, "Why would I want to live forever when I'm not even feeling good now?" But the only way to feel *really* good is to give up the death urge, to begin truly to love life. Others feel they're doing just fine but await a glorious hereafter. Imagine how much *more* spectacular life might be if we don't postpone real living. Death is no solution. Spiritualists claim death doesn't change the vibration of consciousness, which seeks its own level, here or in the hereafter.

What if both of you could become ageless as a couple, and live together as long as you wanted—even hundreds of years! Accepting this possibility and clearing your thinking to actualize it will give your relationship a whole new vibration of sheer vitality. The sacredness increases also because life is God; so more life equals more holiness! When a couple strives for this expression of the Divine, they each become strong and healthy. They truly discover what life is at its best.

THE DEATH URGE IN RELATIONSHIPS

The death urge is the secret or suppressed wish to die. It is not a natural urge, but one created in the human mind. In my other books, I have written about the unconscious urge to die and how it can affect us physically: the body will quite literally self-destruct if this urge is not dealt with directly. In addition, this same impulse can affect your personal interactions, "killing off" your relationships if you aren't careful.

The unconscious death urge originated eons ago when we decided we were separate from God. All disharmony stems from this separation, which is the ultimate self-punishment. The concept of separateness is also an integral part of the belief system that considers death as inevitable.

The death urge can be an outgrowth of religious, family, and societal programming on death or our actual experiences with the death of a loved one. It may stem from our anger and rejection of life or a combination of these factors. The urge to die is present in any anti-life thought. It may manifest itself in an obvious way, or it may assume the disguise of religious doctrine—for example, the belief that heaven is elsewhere—so that death becomes desirable or attractive.

A Course in Miracles sees death as a result of *a thought called the ego,* just as life springs from *a thought called God* (Text, p. 388). God did not create death; we did. And we have nurtured it with lifetimes of accumulated negative thinking.

From early childhood we've been told about our *soul's* potential immortality. The idea that our body also has the potential to regenerate itself is never considered, even though Jesus *does say* "The power of life and death are in the tongue." Because we have the ability to live forever, all death is actually suicide. I cover the subject of physical immortality at length in my book *How to Be Chic and Fabulous and Live Forever* and recommend that you read it. Here, however, I want to discuss the death urge and how it affects our relationships.

Most people slowly kill themselves each day simply by thinking that "death is inevitable." Once established in our minds, this idea is projected onto our relationships with others, as well. Because of this thought, every couple must go through what we call the "death urge of the relationship" sooner or later. We can see this process in action; either one or both of the partners insidiously destroys the relationship—often without even knowing it. Though the partners may or may not be aware of these destructive acts, a conscious third person observing the pair can point out many ways in which the couple is killing off the relationship.

Some individuals act out the death urge within their own bodies, creating illnesses. Others sabotage their careers. Some act it out in their relationships, tearing them apart, and others in all three areas, demolishing everything they have.

It's not difficult to figure out when your own death urge is surfacing. Everything just starts dying on you. Your plants may wither, pets may grow old, your appliances begin to break down, your car conks out, your body falls apart, and you may also feel depressed, moody, or really sick.

Occasionally, none of these symptoms appear because you've suppressed your urge to die. You may be the kind of person who acts your death urge out in one area only—your relationships. These people generally have a hard time coping when their death urge shows up. Their bonds suffer and disintegrate. Others have learned better ways of handling it. If you catch the death urge as it surfaces and deal with it, you can delay the danger until help is available. At this juncture, it would be advisable to take relationship seminars or go on spiritual retreats. Also, I would recommend reading *A Course in Miracles*. You need spiritual purification during this time and you need to stick with it!

In our daily interactions, there are a number of ways that we kill off the vitality of our relationships. These can be corrected if we are vigilant.

- Not being in present time
- Not being spiritually awake or nourished
- Buying into prophesies of doom
- Failing to express our creativity
- Expressing constant put downs and disapproval
- Failure to forgive
- Stuffing our feelings
- Addictions
- Stuffing food, getting fat
- Control and dependency
- Giving away our power

Some relationships that survive the death urge frankly shouldn't. At times, divorce is actually a positive move. When a partnership has become spiritually bankrupt, it may be time to release it. And, obviously, if you or your children are being harmed psychically or physically, you must consider separation.

As a rule, divorce is a personal decision. Even as a counselor, I'm not the one to decide if people should stay together. When I see couples who are in doubt, I usually offer a special prayer: "I pray for this relationship to be healed or for something better for both of us." This way, either decision is a win situation.

There *are* times when a relationship is already dead by the time a couple seeks help, and the partners simply don't have enough desire to resurrect it. But more often I see that people really want to stay together and are simply coping with the death urge in their relationship. If so, we can help them through it.

If you and your partner truly want to be together, yet it feels like your relationship is dying, you should definitely consult with someone who understands how the unconscious death urge operates. I would recommend that you see a rebirther or consultant who has already cleared their own death urge. Ideally, they will understand physical immortality and know that death is not necessary. An immortalist will remind you that out of the great light of God came the spark that was human life. This spark has the same energy and intelligence and power as God. You can recapture that spark and use its Infinite Intelligence to renew your life urge.

This is the time you really need help to draw on that inner power, that eternal God power, returning to a state of harmony with your inner guidance. Such rebalancing often happens during meditation or right in the middle of a rebirthing session. I've seen people pump out streams of negative energy from their death urge in one such session.

Allow those around you—plant, animal, and human—to live. And allow your relationships to live as well. Constantly increase the vitality in your body and in your relationships, and do so with clear principles.

In mortal relationships where both partners are convinced that death is inevitable, their union is governed by fear, urgency, mistrust, and the constant worry, "When is this person going to die and leave me?" When they both work on the elimination of their death urges and are becoming immortals, relationships improve dramatically. Immortal relationships are governed by love, safety, joy, trust, and abundance of time. There is a pervasive sense of well-being and a magic that is undeniable.

When two people know that the choice to keep living is theirs, then unlimited possibilities unfold. But you really have to want immortality to attain it. You have to want to break the cycle fueled by anti-life thought patterns. If your life isn't working, you'll have no desire to live forever, yet the reason it isn't working is that you're not convinced that you really want to live!

Some of us simply cannot tolerate the possibility of physical immortality because we cannot bear the excitement. What path will you choose? The options are there, but the decision is your own.

PHYSICAL IMMORTALITY

I know of nothing that will revitalize a relationship like the goal of physical immortality. Most people feel unsettled by the idea of living forever, and the concept may even strike them as "anti-spiritual," since it differs so markedly from traditional church doctrine. Nothing could be further from the truth. Life is sacred. When you choose more life, you become holier. Such a choice is absolutely spiritual.

In my book *How to Be Chic, Fabulous, and Live Forever,* I discuss physical immortality at length. The title was deliberately chosen to wake up readers and to make it fashionable to think about and discuss immortality. Other immortalists, such as Anna Lee Skarin, are also breaking ground in this debate. Skarin, an Immortal Master who can dematerialize and rematerialize at will, champions the sacred gift of life in her book *The Celestial Song of Creation* (she is also the author of *Beyond Mortal Boundaries*):

Death itself begins with the cells and the tissues as they are gradually undermined and destroyed by the vibrations of all negative evil thoughts and fears. Death comes because the individual himself relinquishes the gift of life. He permits the life force to be crowded out by his own tired, resentful, self-pitying thoughts; his negative attitudes, degenerative desires and greedy actions. Every discordant negative word and attitude are but destructive forces of death bombarding the life of man. The life principle is gradually crowded out and defeated by man's ignorance.

The gift of life is exalted and increased through joy, right thinking, and the positive force of right action. Skarin goes on to explain that as the sacred life force increases, old age and physical deterioration ends. They are conquered as the cells of the body are spiritualized and released from death. This is what the Bible calls "overcoming"—death is automatically conquered through the exaltation of love, praise, and gratitude.

Remember that every individual resides within the vibrations of his own thoughts and mental habits. Vibrations of ecstasy and inner praise nurture the vibration of light. We may choose life over death at any time.

What might be blocking you from making this choice? If you knew you could live forever in your physical body without dying, would you be pleased? If not, your life probably matches one of the following descriptions:

- You're neither enjoying daily existence, nor "winning" at the game of life.
- Your daily life is fine, yet you still believe there is a "higher place."

If you fall into the first category, you'll ask, "Why would I want to live forever when I'm not even feeling good now?" A very good question, and yet its answer reveals a paradox: The only way to feel *really* good is to give up the death urge, to begin to truly love life so much that you would be thrilled at the idea of living forever! This is one of the most important secrets of being happy and healthy.

If you fall into the second category—you're doing well enough, but are waiting for a glorious hereafter—imagine how much *more* spectacular life might be if you stop clinging to the belief that somewhere else is better. Death is no solution; it doesn't necessarily take you to a higher place once you've released your body. As Ruby Nelson tells us in *The Door of Everything*:

> When one chooses to die, death does release the weight of gravity and temporarily frees the soul from earth. But it does not change the vibration of consciousness from the human level. There is no escape from the vibration of yourself except through practiced change of thoughts. Nor does death cause the released consciousness to go to a celestial level. Consciousness, when departing from the body, automatically seeks its own level.
>
> Every lifetime is a new opportunity to be enlightened and anointed with the light and to rise above the trap of death. For he that is joined to Him that is immortal, will also himself become Immortal.

Notice that Ruby Nelson talks about *choosing* to die. This issue is the key: our belief systems determine our reality. What we believe to be true, we create. Though we've been led to believe otherwise, death is a *choice*. Death is therefore optional.

We must become aware of how the death urge, evident in any anti-life thought, pervades every aspect of our life. The fact that our body may feel perfectly healthy right now doesn't necessarily mean we have "handled" physical immortality. Our death urge may very well be suppressed, or we may be acting it out in other areas of our life. Ultimately, this destructive urge is the root cause of everything in your life that isn't working. It is supported by the following actions and thought patterns:

- Invalidation of personal divinity
- Lack of immortalist philosophy
- Belief systems fostering disease
- False religious doctrine
- Family tradition
- Overeating and other addictions
- Unresolved tension and birth trauma

The death urge saps vitality and impairs our judgment. We see this destructive impulse surfacing in many aspects of our society. Observing this phenomenon, my friend Leonard Orr has pointed out the danger inherent in electing old men—whose proximity to death heightens their paranoia—to political office. When the death urge dominates a personality, it blocks out wisdom and inhibits creativity.

War itself is the most obvious and destructive manifestation of the death urge, and dismantling our pro-death mentality will be the key to a lasting peace. Disarmament movements that underestimate the effects of this mentality will last only temporarily. Those that unravel the birth/death cycle will endure, contributing to a *solution* to our greatest social and political problems.

Truly, the fusion of body and spirit united in service creates peace. And because Spirit cannot be destroyed, we, too, cannot be stopped if we keep a clear mind and refuse to indulge in ideologies of separation. The traditional path encouraged us to achieve peace and resolve conflicts, whether personal and global, through control and manipulation. Clearly, this method has proven disastrous. Only understanding the death urge will a new way reveal itself and remove fear from our consciousness.

Some critics say that the idea of physical immortality constitutes ultimate self-aggrandizement. Quite frankly, if immortalists were merely striving to live out an endless, purposeless existence, I would agree with them. But this is not the case. The real passion for immortality grows out of a selfless dedication to divine service. As one proponent described it, physical immortality is "a condition of maximum efficiency for achieving the true goal of assisting in the world of creation."

Robert Coon, my consultant on this subject, believes that we must take a vow dedicating our will to the attainment of physical immortality. This vow includes a commitment to living fully; it means not letting anything come between us and our spirituality and consciously letting go of our false religious beliefs. We must dispense with the myth that we are separate from God, that we die and go to heaven, and that God determines when we should die.

In my books I have mentioned that aging is controlled by consciousness. Astrologer Linda Goodman's adage, "No anger, no rage, no age!" neatly expresses this concept. She also talks about the body being a self-regenerating battery. You can't exaggerate the importance of knowing that this is the truth. You can't just *believe* in it—such ideas lie beyond all belief systems. You have to know it in your bones.

Once you've relinquished your negative religious programming and committed yourself to living fully, you should communicate the truth of everlasting life in your own creative way. You yourself can help resurrect our universe from death.

It is valuable to learn the wisdom of immortals on all of the subjects they write and talk about. Study Linda Goodman's steps toward physical immortality and other books on this subject. Before closing, I want to share this wonderful piece by Haridas Chaudhuri, from his book *Being, Evolution and Immortality:*

PHYSICAL IMMORTALITY: THE ULTIMATE PHASE OF INITIATION

Finally, the concept of immortality implies a harmonization of the entire personality and a transformation of the physical organism as an effective channel of expression of higher values. This may be called material immortality (*rupaniar mukti*).

There are some mystics and spiritual seekers who strengthen and purify their bodies just enough to be able to experience the thrilling touch of the Divine. They use the body as a ladder, which by climbing, the pure spiritual level—the domain of immortality—is to be reached. On attaining that level, the body is felt as a burden, as a prison house, as a string of chains that holds one in bondage.

Dissociation from this last burden of the body is considered a sine qua non for complete liberation. Continued association with the body is believed to be the result of the last lingering trace of ignorance (*avidya leia*). When the residual trace of ignorance is gone, the spirit is finally set free from the shackles of the body.

The above view is based upon a subtle misconception about the purpose of life and the significance of the body. The body is not only a ladder that leads to the realm of immortality, but also an excellent instrument for expressing the glory of immortality in life and society. It is capable of being thoroughly penetrated by the light of the spirit. It is capable of being transformed into what has been called the "Diamond Body." As a result of such transformation, the body does not appear any more to be a burden upon the liberated self. On the contrary, it becomes a perfect image of the self. It shines as the Spirit made flesh. It functions as a very effective instrument for creative action and realization of higher values in the world. It is purged of all inner tension and conflict. It is liberated from the anxiety of all repressed wishes. It is also liberated from the dangerous grip of the death impulse born of self-repression. Mystics who look upon the body as a burden suffer from the anxiety of self-repression and the allurement of the death wish.

Material immortality means decisive victory over both of these demons. It conquers the latent death instinct in man, and fortifies the will to live as long as necessary, as a channel of expression of the Divine. It also liquidates all forms of self-suppression and self-torture and self-mutilation. As a result of the total being of an individual becomes strong and steady, whole and healthy. There is a free flow of psychic energy. It is increasingly channeled into ways of meaningful self-expression. Under the guidance of the indwelling light of the eternal, it produces increasing manifestation of the spirit in matter.

THE IMMORTAL COUPLE AS A NEW PARADIGM

Instead of getting old together and dying, imagine the opposite. What if both of you could become ageless as a couple, and live together as long as you wanted—even hundreds of years! Sounds farfetched? Not anymore. We now have the knowledge to make this happen. Deepak Chopra is writing and lecturing on the subject of physical immortality and backing it up scientifically.

An immortal is a soul who has already experienced enough male and female incarnations that the birth/death cycle can now be transcended; this soul can stay here to serve as long as it chooses.

In order for a couple to become immortal, they obviously have to work out their "unconscious death urge." This is an incredible subject for a couple to study together. You have to master the philosophy, psychology, and physiology of the unconscious.

What this does for a relationship is simply incredible. The relationship takes on a whole new vibration of sheer vitality. The sacredness increases also because life is God; and so more life equals more holiness! When two immortals are together, there is a sense of well-being that pervades the underlying structure of the relationship. I've seen relationships in which each person is constantly dealing with suppressed fear, such as when is this other person going to leave or die? Also, a typical couple usually projects the unconscious death urge onto the relationship: The tendency is to kill it off in insidious ways.

Many people cannot tolerate the idea of physical immortality because it is too exciting! They might be addicted to pain and struggle. Others simply don't want to live forever in a physical body because they hate their life! (They don't know that one of the reasons their life doesn't work is because they haven't cleared their death urge.) As *A Course in Miracles* states, "Death is a result of the thought called the ego, just as surely as life is a result of the thought called God." Understanding this point is imperative.

When a couple strives for this expression of the Divine, they each become strong and healthy; there is a miraculous and free flow of psychic energy. This energy can then be channeled into meaningful self-expression. When a couple expresses together the glory of immortality into their life and society, they function as effective instruments for creative action and a realization of higher values in the world. They truly discover what life is at its best, and they are willing and happy to share their blossoming emotional and sexual relationship.

INDEX

A

The Abundance Book (Price), 111, 121
Abusive relationships, 153
Acceptance, 180
Active listening, 88–89
Adjustments in relationships, 32–34
Affairs, 190
Affirmations of forgiveness, 98
Aging, 223–224
Alienation and marriage, 129–130
Aliveness quotient, 114
Altar, 128, 164
Anger
  and aging, 223–224
  birth experience and, 20
  A Course in Miracles on, 53, 64–65
  dangers of, 59
  defending anger, 59–60
  encouragement of, 63
  humor defusing, 63–64
  mixed messages about, 81
  money and, 122
Apologies, 162
Arguelles, José, 14, 22
Arguments, prevention of, 61
Ascension attitudes, 23, 83–84, 163
Attracting mates, 35–36

B

Babaji, 93, 140, 150–151
  and Divine Love, 209
  on forgiveness, 160
  on service, 171–172, 193
Balance, sense of, 30–31
Being, Evolution and Immortality (Chaudhuri), 224–226
Beyond God the Father (Daly), 30

Beyond Mortal Boundaries (Skarin), 219–220
The Bible, viii
  and blessing, 163–165
  on death and overcoming, 220
  on devotion, 185
  on life, 214
  and purification, 23
Birth experience, 19–20
Bitterness and letting go, 150–152
Blame, 1–2
  blessing and, 184–185
  conflict and, 181–182
  as distraction, 94–95
  enlightenment and, 49
Blessing, 154
  blame and, 184–185
  and judging, 163–165
  situations for, 164–165
Bliss, 154, 168–169
Body, significance of, 225
Breaking up, 148–149

C

Car, neatness of, 116
Carey, Ken, 8
Caring for relationships, 105–108
The Celestial Song of Creation (Skarin), 219–220
Change
  A Course in Miracles on, 186
  fear of, 144–147
  and purification, 93
Chaudhuri, Haridas, 224–226
The Child of Your Dreams (Huxley), 134
Children, 134–138
  spiritual environment and, 112–113
Choosing to die, 221–222
Chopra, Deepak, 106, 226

Clean wave form, 14, 22
Clearing relationships, 54–55, 90–93, 99–104, 109–110
  supporting persons in, 101–102
  unwillingness to clear, 100–101
  and upsets, 158
Clinton, Bill, 50–51
Clinton, Hillary, 50–51
Co-dependent bargaining, 205
Communication, 77–79
  double messages, 80–82
  and relationship dynamics, 72
  techniques for, 78–79
Community of majesty, 191–192
Competition, 14
Confessing your case, 83
Conflict
  alleviation of, 193
  A Course in Miracles on, 181–183
  money conflicts, 119–122
  resolution techniques, 103
  and sex, 112
  and stuck relationships, 91
Conforming, 85–86
Confusion
  about God, 3
  highest spiritual thought and, 57–58
  power struggle and, 31
Consciousness and death, 221
Coon, Robert, 223
Coppola, Eleanor, 51
Correction, 180
Cosmic ties, 43
A Course in Miracles, viii, 2, 10
  on anger, 53, 59–60, 64–65
  on clearing relationships, 103–104
  on conflict, 181–183
  on death, 215, 227

dedication of relationships to
God, 7
and Divine Self, 195–196
enlightenment defined, 48–49
on forgiveness, 160
on guilt, 96
and Highest Reality, 212
on intimacy, 189
on knowing ourselves, 74–75
on life, 213–214
on love, 160, 185–186, 208
and sacred relationships, 12
and self-pity, 152
on sexual matters, 127–128
on sharing, 187–188
Sonship concept in, 177–178
special hate relationships, 209
on special relationships, 170,
173
and stuck relationships, 90
on upsets, 153, 158
on victims, 30
Crises in relationships, 46–47
Criticism, 145, 154
Culture and monogamy, 190

D

Daily maintenance of relationships, 54–55
Daly, Mary, 30
Death urge, 111
acting out of, 216
choosing to die, 221–222
immortal relationship,
213–227
overcoming, viii
in relationships, 214–219
sex and, 128
Debts, karmic, 156
Defenses, 205
Denial, 107
Dependency, 13, 20
Devotion, 166–167
The Bible on, 185

*The Dialogue on Conscious
Education* (Grant), 135
Diamond Body, 225
Difficulties in relationships,
141–143
Disagreements, 52
Discarding old models, 25–26
Discourses (Meher Baba),
156–157, 169
Divine Control, 196, 206–207
Divine Love, 196, 208–210
Divine Mother, 192, 195, 199
Divine Self, 195–196
Divine substance, 111
Divorce as positive, 217
The Door of Everything
(Nelson), 23, 83, 221
Double messages, 80–82
Dovetailing patterns, 141
Drinking the Divine (Ray), 212
Dues, karmic, 156
Dynamics of relationships,
72–73

E

Ego
and bliss, 168–169
crises of, 211–212
dissolution of, 9–10
enlightenment and, 48–49
expression of, 182
illusion of, 74–76
marriage and, 133
as mistaken identity, 196–197
peace and, 61, 183–184
separation and, 211
transience of, 202–203
Ego Mind, 202
Egotism, 18
Encouragement, 204–205
Ending relationships, 148–149
and bitterness, 150–152
Energy in relationships, 41–42
Enlightenment, 2

achieving, 5–6, 48–49
approaches to, 147
of Whole Woman, 198
Entrapment, fear of, 13, 20
Equality, achievement of, 27–29
Errors, acknowledgment of, 82
*The Esoteric Philosophy of
Love and Marriage*
(Fortune), 42
Essays on Sacred Relationships
(Ray), vi, vii
Extended family, 192

F

Failed relationships, 149
Faith
and letting go, 183
mind tracks and, 68
False motives, 193–194
Fate, 156
Fear
of change, 144–147
of equality, 27–29
of intimacy, 190
of pleasure, 13, 20
Feedback, 123–126
giving feedback, 124–125
receiving feedback, 125
Feelings
mistaken attribution of,
182–183
releasing unpleasant feelings,
62
Feminism, 14, 31
First-aid for relationships,
141–143
Forgiveness
affirmations for, 98
and guilt, 91, 97
power for, 179
and unconscious behavior,
160
Formaini, Helen, 190
Fortune, Dion, 42, 43

Foundation for Inner Peace, viii

G

Giving thanks, 83
God
  clearing relationship with, 3–4
  as highest reality, 211–212
  purpose of life and, 9
  relationship to, 1–2
  separateness from, 203
  Sonship, 172–173
God-realized Self, 212
Goodman, Linda, 223–224
Grant, Margaret, 135
Gratitude, 204–205
Greed, 120
Grieving period, 152
Growth and relationships, 11
Guilt, 90–91
  conflict and, 181–182
  giving up, 96–97
  money and, 122
  serial monogamy and, 146

H

Habits, 69, 118
Harmony, 52
Hate relationship, 164–1657
Hating yourself, 15–16
Healing relationships, 105–108
Healing yourself, 15–16
Highest reality, 211–212
Highest spiritual thought, 56–58
Holy relationships, 132–133, 173–176
Home
  maintenance of, 111, 117
  self-esteem and, 114–118
Honesty, 110
How to Be Chic, Fabulous, and Live Forever (Ray), 215, 219

How to Raise a Child of God (Singh), 136–137
How to Spiritualize Your Marriage (Kruyananda), 130
Humor, anger and, 63–64
Huxley, Laura, 134

I

Ideal Birth (Ray), 134
Immortal relationship, 213–227
Incest taboo pattern, 45–46
Inner peace, symptoms of, 66
Innocence, forgiveness and, 97
Inspiration and devotion, 185
Intent magazine, 41–42
Interviewing
  potential partners, 32–33
  process, 39–40
  sex and, 12
Intimacy
  with everyone, 189–190
  fear of, 190
  as path, 11–12
Intuition, 198
"I" sentences, 110
Isolation, safety in, 190

J

Jacobson, Bonnie, 53, 65
Jesus, 17
  and Divine Love, 209
  on forgiveness, 97
  on immortality of soul, 215
  on reincarnation, 155
Joy, 2, 9, 220
Judging
  blessing and, 163–165
  yourself, 152

K

Kahunas, 154
Karma, 2, 155–157
  law of, 193
  purpose of life and, 9
  relationships based on, 42–43

Karma Yoga, 9, 193
Kruyananda, Swami, 130

L

Laschelles, Diana, 146
Learning, 9
Letting go, 183
Life, gift of, 220
Listening, active, 88–89
Loss, focus on, 84
Love
  A Course in Miracles and, 185–186
  crisis and, 47
  definition of, 13
  Divine Love, 196, 208–210
  fear of, 20
  self-approval, 13, 17
  self-love, 15–16
  sexual love, 127
Loving Relationships (Ray), vi–vii
Loving Relationships II (Ray), vi, vii
Loving Relationships Training workshop, vi

M

Marriage, 129–133
  ego relationships, 133
  God in, 112
  holy/unholy relationships, 132–133
  matching planes and, 43
  rebirthing and abusive marriage, 159–160
Masculinity, models of, 25
Material immortality, 224–225
Mature love, 47
Meditation
  and children, 134, 136
  and guilt, 97
Meher Baba, 155–156, 169, 194
  on love, 209
"Men hurt me" belief, 5–6

Mind
  Ego Mind, 202
  enlightenment and, 49
  state of mind, 87–88
Mind tracks, 67–71
Mission in relationship, 50–51
Mistaken attribution of feelings, 182–183
Mixed messages, 80–82
Money, 112, 119–122
  co-dependent bargaining, 205
  desire and, 194
  respect and, 162
Money rejection complex, 120
Monogamy, 190

N
Nagging, 79
Neatness, 114–118
Negative thoughts, 1–2
  birth experiences and, 5
Nelson, Ruby, 23, 83, 221
New Relationships Training
  workshop, vi
New sex, 127–128
*A New Vision for Women's
  Liberation* (Rajneesh), 130

O
Ohana, 192
Old models, discarding, 25–26
Old sex, 127–128
Om Namaha Shivaia, 93
Oneness with God, 4
Openness to relationships,
  35–36
Open relationships, 190
Orgasm, 127
Orr, Leonard, 48, 158–159, 222
Other Lives, Other Selves
  (Woolger), 9, 43, 135
Over-processing habit, 101

P
Pain
  denial and, 107

ending relationships and, 148
Path, stages of, 169
Patriarchy, 25–26
Patterns in relationships, 45–47
Peace, 60–61
  ego as obstacle to, 183–184
  mixed messages about, 81
  symptoms of inner peace, 66
Peace, Love and Healing
  (Siegal), 66
Peace Corps, 172, 194
Peck, Scott, 31
Perceiving ourselves, 74–76
Perfection, 158–159
Pettiness, 82
Phases of relationship, 32–34
Physical healing, 106
Physical immortality, 219–226
Pitman, Frank, 25
Plato, 208
Play, 136
Pleasure, fear of, 13, 20
Ponder, Catherine, 83
Positive, stating the, 107–108
Power. *See also* Equality
  fear of, 14
  imbalance of, 201
  of Whole Woman, 199
Praise
  focusing on, 163–164
  habit of, 154
  saturation, 165
Pre- and Perinatal Psychology
  Association of N.A., 135
Pre-/perinatal psychology,
  134–135
Price, John Randolph, 121
Principle of right association, 169
Problem-solving, 59–66
  active listening, 88–89
  in New Paradigm, 87–89
  processes for, 73
  state of mind for, 87–88
Projecting, 94
Pure Joy (Ray), 8, 191

Purification, 22–24
  chanting and, 93
Purpose
  of life, 9–10
  of relationships, 1–2

Q
Quantum Healing (Chopra),
  106

R
Rajneesh, Bhagwan, 112, 127,
  130
Ram Dass, 2, 8
Reality
  creating alternative, 68
  highest reality, 211–212
  True Reality, 202
Rebelling, 85–86
Rebirthing, 13, 19–21, 48
  and abusive marriage,
  159–160
  fear and, 145
Reincarnation, 155–157
Relationship history, 39–40
Relationships technology, 192
Releasing feelings, 62
Respect, 161–162
Responsibility, 94–95
  for upsets, 159
Right association, principle of,
  169

S
Sacred partnerships, 2, 11–12
Saibaba, 8
Salvation, hope of, 174
Samadhi, 127, 168
Samskaras, 193
Secret affairs, 190
*The Secret Life of the Unborn
  Child* (Verny), 134
Self-aggrandizement, 223
Self-esteem, 18
  grieving and, 152

Self-esteem, continued
  and home, 114–118
  and intuition, 198
  men and, 31
  physical surroundings and,
    111
  in weakening relationships,
    70
Self-hatred, 15–16
Self-image, 20
Self-improvement, 159
Selfless service, 171–172,
    193–194
Self-love, 13, 17–18
Separation
  avoidance of, 177–178
  concept of separateness, 215
  and crisis, 178
  ego and, 211
Separation anxiety, 13, 20
Serial monogamy, 139–140,
    146–147
Service
  life of, 193–194
  purpose of life and, 9
  selfless service, 171–172,
    193–194
Sex, 127–128
  birth experience and, 20
  conflicts over, 112
  interviewing before, 12
  judgment and desire, 42
Sharing, 187–188
Shastriji, 23
Siegal, Bernie, 66
Sin, 96
Singh, Tara, 136–137
Skarin, Anna Lee, 219–220
Smoking, 159–160, 205
Sonship, 172–173, 177–178
  limiting of, 189
Soul
  immortality of, 215
  unity, 131
Special hate relationships, 209

Spiritual dynamics, 153–154
Spiritual missions, 50–51
Spiritual relationships, 170–172
Spiritual teamwork, 26
State of mind, 87–88
Strengthening relationships, 41
  development of, 70–71
Stuck relationships, 90–91
Summers, Marshall, 18
Suppression of death urge, 222
Surfers of the Uvula
    (Arguelles), 22
Surrender, 202–203
Sutphen, Dick, 9, 42–43

T

Task Force on Conscious
    Education, 135
Tension
  lessening tension, 63
  in marriage, 44
Terra Christa, the Global
    Spiritual Awakening
    (Carey), 8
Thanks, giving, 83
Thought. See also Negative
    thoughts
  and children, 137
  highest spiritual thought,
    56–58
Tillet, Rob, 41–42
Transitioning relationships,
    139–140
Transmuting upsets, 158–160
True Reality, 202
Truth
  communication of, 78
  special relationships and, 175

U

Unconscious behavior, 153,
    158–160
Unholy relationships, 132–133,
    173–176
Upsets

A Course in Miracles on, 153
  respect and, 161–162
  transmuting, 158–160

V

Vaughan, 212
Verny, Thomas, 134
Vibrations of life, 220
Victims, 30
Vision of relationship, 37–38

W

Walsh, 212
War and death urge, 222–223
Weakening relationships, 41–42
  destructive behaviors in,
    69–70
We Were Born Again to Be
    Together (Sutphen), 9,
    42–43
Whittaker, Terry Cole, 8
Whole Woman, 195–197,
    198–199
Williamson, Marianne, 152
Wisdom and death urge, 222
"Women suffocate me" belief,
    6
Wooler, Vicki, 89
Woolger, Roger, 9, 43, 135
Worship, 166–167
Writing and stuck relation-
    ships, 92–93

Y

Yelling, 65
Yogananda
  and Divine Love, 209–210
  on Divine Mother, 195, 200
  on faults, 205
  on marriage, 131
  on reincarnation, 155
Yogis, 200

Z

Zitko, 127